PRAISE

Nicely done. Easy reading and informative. — E. Antonio Mangu-bat, MD

Hormones have been the key to keeping my brain working and my health. Such an important thing you are doing. — *June*

I can't tell you how many people are SHOCKED that I have survived 8 years of hormone treatment and not grown an extra head or died of cancer. — *Sandi*

Wow. I wish I had this information when I was 40. Because of reading the book combined with feeling crummy, I started taking 2 thyroid (1 grain) and 2 estradiol (1 mg) per day, 2 progesterone (200 mg), and a bunch of testosterone cream. I feel better now, but not as good as when I had the testosterone pellet. — *Leslie S.*

You've done more for me than I can say. I can't believe I'm almost 60 and feel so good. I'm on a swim team and do triathlons and still like

sex. My friends my age are not so lucky. And I know it's because of you. — Cindy R.

I read your book over and over as I learn more about my hormones. I've been on estrogen, testosterone, thyroid, progesterone, and HGH I get from South America. It all makes me feel great, very sexual and I run marathons. — Jan, 58 years old

Thank you for sharing this Hormone book! I am suffering from a drastic hormone shift, so this is extremely valuable to me! Although I have desired HRT for some time, I am advised that it is a dangerous thing and the risks of cancer and heart disease accompany that option. I look forward to reading this book.

I am grateful for the opportunity to have been able to listen to your podcast about Butchered by Healthcare. As I listened, with horror, I could not help but be challenged by the grand decisions that I need to make regarding my healthcare, and moreover, the healthcare (that I am constantly arranging) for my seven-year-old granddaughter that I am raising. She was born with fetal alcohol syndrome and suffers from cerebral palsy, a seizure, and a pain disorder. You could probably guess the medications that she is currently prescribed.

I considered myself to be astute and well-read, however, I always regarded the tales of "Big Pharma" as those of conspiracy theorists (somewhat) and was on the fence within my own judgment. You have cleared that up and dispelled that myth. Knowing that it was bold of you to be forthright and very clear to the readers, I pray for your safety!!!! It would be revolutionary for many of your peers in the medical community to come forth with honesty. Do they even have a realization of their enslavement to that machine, or have they taken their oaths and look the other way?!

I am appreciative and supportive of your efforts, honesty, and mission to make "us" aware. (even though now I feel this world is hopelessly doomed to the control of the greedy!). — Susan, 57 years old

HORMONE SECRETS

Feel Great and Age Well Using the Bio-identicals

ROBERT YOHO
ROBERT L. MORGAN

Inverness Press

The stories here came from actual patients or doctors, who all gave permission. I changed some of their names and a few details to preserve their privacy.

COVER CREDITS

I found this original mask in Taquerias Arandas Mexican restaurant in Humble, Texas, near Houston. The design ideas for the cover were mine. The graphic artist who put the image together was Helen Olatunji from Nigeria. The owner kindly gave me permission to use the images.

IN APPRECIATION

Neal Rouzier, MD, pulled together the hormone research of the last four decades and revolutionized therapy. Decades of experience with these patients also informed his teaching. He understood and emphasized the value of estrogen for men and the health problems with estrogen blockers. Neal spent untold hours trying to teach his colleagues that not every case of a high red-cell count was Polycythemia Vera.

Dr. Rouzier conducts seminars worldwide and has trained thousands of physicians about hormone usage. Those of us observing him have been fascinated and occasionally mystified by his Socratic teaching style. I included links to a few of his lectures in the Trusted Resources section. His work is highlighted at worldlinkmedical.com. Around 2015, I changed from Neal's friend into his fan.

Although this material is partially derivative of Dr. Rouzier's efforts, I am solely responsible for any mistakes or misconceptions.

Robert Morgan, APRN, wrote the weight loss chapter and his vast experience advised the rest of this book. He passed away during the final editing. He was a member of every physician hormone group and knew the academics better than anyone but Neal. He was a generous friend who will be deeply missed.

CONTENTS

DISCLAIMER

I have no conflicts of interest that I can identify. I am not solic-
iting business for myself—I retired from practice when I was 66
and resigned my medical license. I had a fantastic career as a
cosmetic surgeon, and I was initially sad to end it. But I am
happy that I have a small part of my life left to write, research,
and contribute.

I have no financial relationship with any doctor or institu-
tion, nor have I received funding from anyone. I own no
substantial healthcare stock. If there are any net profits from this
book, I will donate them to a worthy cause.

These are my opinions based on decades of medical training,
practice, and reading the literature. I make no guarantees about
them, and none of this book should be construed as specific
medical advice. Your licensed providers are the only ones who
should advise you, and you should not treat yourself. In this age
of frivolous lawsuits, I cannot specifically recommend any of the
caregivers mentioned here. Remember that each has an individual license and they, not I, are responsible for your treatment.

My descriptions of steroids and illegally manufactured

substances are accurate as far as I know. However, I recommend against violating any law or using drugs without medical supervision. Ordering medications from other countries may be illegal, but if you have a prescription, prosecution for this is unknown to me as of the publication date.

The standard disclaimer: I supply this book for "entertainment purposes only." This applies to all the material here.

PREFACE

If you do not know by now that corporations have disfigured healthcare, you have been living under a rock. For example, hormone therapy is claimed to be hazardous, but a century's science and experience prove its value. When these natural substances are low or absent, replacing them may be the safest and most effective treatment we have. In contrast, drugs are foreign substances that cause side effects and worse.

Hormone supplementation potentially treats or improves:

Longevity: Low levels of thyroid, growth hormone, estrogen, testosterone, and DHEA (dehydroepiandrosterone) are linked to premature death.

Cancer: Estrogen, DHEA, testosterone, progesterone, melatonin, and human growth hormone (HGH) all have protective effects against cancer.

General health: In women under age 60, long-term estrogen replacement therapy decreases strokes, blood clots, colon cancer, diabetes, and macular degeneration. It reduces the likelihood of tooth loss, depression, osteoporosis, and death because of bone fracture. Breast cancer is unaffected, contrary to common opinion. Avoidance of estrogen was estimated to cause 50,000 excess deaths over ten years in a Yale study.

Alzheimer's disease (AD): When long-term care costs are included, this is the most expensive ailment of all. Estrogen decreases the chances of getting AD significantly when it is started within 10 years of menopause.

Heart disease: Over 40 observational studies have shown that giving estrogen to women reduces coronary artery disease, heart attacks, and deaths. When men have higher levels, they have less heart disease. Giving natural estrogen to deficient men improves cholesterol but does not increase blood clotting.

Depression: Estrogen, DHEA, progesterone, testosterone, and melatonin all have antidepressant effects. Thyroid has been studied and used for depression for over fifty years.

Obesity: Thyroid, estrogen, testosterone, DHEA, and human growth hormone reduce unhealthy belly fat and promote weight loss.

"Bio-identical" hormones are the same as those found in humans. These are safe, affordable, and have few side effects. But since these natural body substances cannot be easily patented, they are barely profitable for big Pharma. So the drugmakers concoct proprietary imitations from chemicals or animals. Their prices are extortionate.

Stories have been spread that hormones such as estrogen and testosterone cause cancer, heart disease, blood clots, and other diseases. With few exceptions, these are false. And for insulin, growth hormone, and others, we have allowed the drugmakers to exorbitantly increase their fees using proprietary manufacturing. The result is that hormones are overpriced and difficult to prescribe. Doctors are pressured to use toxic, expensive patent drugs instead. These trends are squandering our resources and costing us years of healthy life.

PART I
INTRODUCTION

CHAPTER 1
WHY LISTEN TO ME?

I am now retired, but I spent the last thirty years in private practice performing cosmetic surgery and sometimes assisting with my patients' medical care. Most of the women I worked with who were over 50 years old suffered from poor sleep, fatigue, hot flashes, muscle wasting, and irritability. They were all looking for a way to feel better and a lot were taking antidepressants. Many thought that I could improve their spirits with surgery, and sometimes they were right. But since they had hormone deficiency symptoms, surgery alone was not the best solution.

Most plastic surgeons operate on a string of depressed people without considering why they are so miserable. My patients were trusting me, and I wanted to help, so I took training.

For nearly two decades, I offered appropriate candidates hormone treatment along with their procedures. Those who listened to my advice were usually grateful. Some were not interested, and I respected that as well.

I knew women had doubts about hormone replacement. I also knew that patients never take at least a third of their prescriptions, even vital ones like kidney transplant anti-rejection drugs. Since hormone benefits can take weeks to be felt, I used long-lasting, inexpensive testosterone pellets implanted under the skin. If my patients didn't like this idea, I offered it as a cream. Testosterone transforms into estrogen, so they received this as well.

When I saw them a month later, most were thrilled. I then suggested they consider adding progesterone, estrogen, vitamin D, and sometimes thyroid, DHEA, and melatonin. If their finances were tight, I showed them how to inject themselves once a week with testosterone. (Each shot costs only $2 for women and $10 for men.) I followed blood tests, symptoms, and physical exams, and customized therapy based on patient responses.

I saw a few women who felt terrible in their mid-30s. Blood tests showed they were in premature menopause and had estrogen and progesterone levels close to zero. After they began treatment, they felt great again. Many of my patients brought in their friends and husbands, and they responded as well.

Hormone replacement should be a "feel-good" story. We have overwhelming proof that it is safe and effective. Most hormones are affordable, and tens of millions of people have used them. Thyroid has been available since the late 1800s, and insulin, estrogen, and testosterone for nearly that long. These treat or prevent heart disease, depression, impotence, diabetes, some cancers, and Alzheimer's disease (AD).

But misinformation is everywhere:

✪ Doctors and patients "know" that estrogen causes breast cancer and blood clots, testosterone causes heart disease and prostate cancer, and that human growth hormone (HGH) is practically poison. These ideas are false.

✪ We have been led to believe that insulin's high price is justifiable. Wrong.

✪ Mainstream medicine says that thyroid disease is relatively uncommon and hazardous to treat. This is also incorrect— it may afflict a third of mature women and is under-treated because of doctors' economic turf wars rather than unusual risks.

Hormone therapy is a strange opera with many twists and bizarre characters. To navigate it, patients need physician-level knowledge—a tragic situation. I studied this subject for a decade, but you can learn the basics in a few hours with no prior background.

Journalists think every issue has two sides. Law and news stories, for example, are rarely black or white. But medical care is right or wrong, and I challenge you to find the truth here. I present:

✪ What the science says.

✪ Opinions of independent experts.

✪ The collective physician experience of nearly a century.

✪ My patients' opinions about their treatment. Their words are not scholarly, but they are meaningful and convincing.

Scan this QR code with your camera for one of the best
testimonials:

To understand the controversy, you must also learn how the corporations purchased the scientific debate using our public healthcare money. Since then, they have gotten filthy rich peddling questionable drugs for insurance payments. The benefits of hormones for aging were discredited during the same period. The consequence is that we are not using hormones to prevent disease for most of the people who would benefit—at least a quarter of the population. The standard that developed instead was to wait until health declined, then chase the resulting illness using astronomically expensive patent drugs with noxious side effects.

The monstrous economic scrum we call healthcare ruined medical science. The studies about hormones, along with the rest, are stuffed with bias, pretentious jargon, apples-to-oranges comparisons, and complex, dimly understood science. You may initially think they are impossible to interpret and that you cannot come to any conclusions. But if you consider all the evidence, you will see through the fog.

What are my qualifications? Four years ago, when I was 63, I cut my surgical practice to half-time and started researching. I previously thought the Food and Drug Administration (FDA) had integrity, the other healthcare players were principled, and that the medical literature was reliable. I soon understood that finances rule everything and that we have given a blank check to the medical industry. They have become wealthy, arrogantly entitled, and even power-mad. They have acquired the journals and academic medicine and are fabricating medical standards to boost sales. Patients are a distant priority for them.

All the harmful practices and chasing after wealth shocked me. My award-winning book, *Butchered by "Healthcare"* (2020), grew out of my efforts to understand what was occurring. It is the background and companion to this work and will help you fact-check and fill in gaps. My frequent references to it may seem promotional, but trust me—no one makes money on books that expose medical wrongdoing.

This is a podcast introduction.

HEALTHCARE IS A PATCHWORK FRANKENSTEIN'S MONSTER—PART miracle, part corruption, and deformed by commercial interests. Somehow, it still walks, but I cannot put lipstick on it.

Note: I wrote this book with the collaboration of Robert L. Morgan, APRN, a colleague who had a huge hormone practice (I owe you, Robert). I used the first person for easy reading.

Robert Yoho
Pasadena, CA
RobertYohoAuthor.com
June 2021

FOR POWER READERS

✪ Skip or scan anything that is too technical for you and browse out-of-order based on your gender and interests.

✪ Delay studying healthcare corruption until you understand hormone basics. Medical care is a pay-to-play industry infested by misconduct, and seeing how bad it is can be overwhelming.

✪ The e-book has links to references. The Resources section has hundreds more and some lectures.

✪ To convince you I did not cherry-pick sources to manufacture conclusions, Appendix C has over 50 references about a narrow but pivotal area—the prevention of Alzheimer's disease with hormones. I could have done this for any topic in this book.

✪ Try not to feud with me over small trees in this forest. If some disagreement kidnaps you and you quit reading, you will lose your chance to understand the ecosystem.

Three "Blue's Clues"—practical rules of thumb—will help you interpret science writing.

✪ If you do not follow the reasoning, it is likely a lie used to sell something. You are as smart as the storyteller, so do not let them fool you. (This also applies to lawyers and financial advisors.) Never be seduced by detail at the expense of your intuition.

✪ The updated Golden Rule: Those with the gold make the rules, so finding the funding source is telling. If you consult outside references, you will find the sponsors at the end of each paper. Their ethics may not pass a sniff test.

✪ Controversy, confusion, and extravagant claims about small numbers prove that *whatever it is does not work.* Never fall into the trap of believing, "reasonable people disagree" or "the science is developing."

Although academics deride Wikipedia, it might be the most reliable remaining medical information source. But never forget that it is under constant attack by industry ghostwriters.

Not even China, whose leaders try to rewrite history, can hide from web crawlers. Although ten percent of links disappear every year because of "link rot," virtually everything that was ever seen on the Web is still alive and well on the Wayback Machine Internet archive. Just copy the bad link (the web address at the top of the browser) and enter it at archive.org. Then look for the backed-up copies and select the date to review. You can also save any URL free at another of their pages. These

are Internet superpowers that are handy to have in your
bookmarks.

I cite some references that are behind paywalls, but blasting
through most of these is easy. If you copy the link into the Sci-
hub.st website browser, you can download academic articles
free. This is a piracy website based in Russia and using it is
against the law, so I give you this information for "entertainment purposes" only. But some academics publicly thank
the Hub.

CHAPTER 2
LEARN A FEW DRUG NAMES

To understand this book, you only need to remember a few bio-identical hormone names—*estradiol, progesterone, testosterone, and thyroids, which include porcine, T4, and T3.* If you read outside sources, you must learn others. Return to this reference chapter as needed.

HORMONES WORK BY ATTACHING TO RECEPTOR MOLECULES IN THE human body, and since the natural ones are identical or nearly identical to those made by our glands, they fit like the real thing. Manufactured medicines are foreign substances never found in the body's ecosystem that are made from animals or chemicals. These do not match as closely as the bio-identicals, do not work as well, and have side effects. They are still useful in a few circumstances but should never be taken long-term. I call them "counterfeit" or "fake" to help you sort out the issues.

For example, progesterone is bio-identical. In contrast, Provera is a synthetic progesterone imitation. It raises the chances of migraines, weight gain, heart disease, breast cancer, depression, and irregular bleeding. Pregnant women taking it get more miscarriages and their babies have more congenital disabilities.

BETTER: HUMAN BIO-IDENTICALS	UNDESIRABLE: FAKES FROM PHARMA
ESTRADIOL (patch, pill, cr) Climera, Vivelle Dot patches (brands) Compounded cream and pills	Premarin, Ogen etc. made from horse urine
PROGESTERONE (pill, inj, cream) Prometrium 100 mg (branded, this dose only) Compounded pills, injection (Compounded cream, weak)	Provera, other "progestins:" chemicals related to progesterone.
TESTOSTERONE, cream, pellets, injectable; generics, compounded. Brands: AndroGel/derm cream, Natesto nasal gel, Testopel pellet, others. Bio-identical.	Testosterones are bio-identical, but most proprietary brands use low doses that barely work
THYROID, pork (Armour, Naturethroid and others) Has both T3 and T4. Works better for many.	Levothyroxine/ Synthroid (and others, T4 only) May not work as well but OK for many people.

Drugmakers invent sexy copyrighted brand names for their profitable patented compounds. This allows patients to harass doctors by saying, "I saw an ad for…" Pharma also creates chemical names that are hard to pronounce and remember. The brand Celebrex, for example, is the chemical celecoxib—try saying that one. The advantage for the manufacturer is that when medications go off patent and are sold as generics, the chemical is more difficult to recall than the recognizable brand.

The drugmakers use the names to confuse. Progestin, progestogen, and Provera, the artificial ones, sound like natural progesterone. And Premarin, the horse-urine estrogen (this name was from PRegnant MAre's uRINe), gets mixed up with Provera, the synthetic progesterone. These strategies work, so the doctors are just as bewildered as you are:

✪ Many journal articles make no distinction between bio-identical progesterone and progestins/progestogens such as Provera. They call both of these "progesterone," which implies there is little difference.

✪ Likewise, medical articles call many related substances estrogens, which is accurate but fools both doctors and patients into thinking that they are all alike. Technically, estrogens include bio-identical estradiol, the counterfeits such as Premarin, and the other relatively weak human estrogens, estrone and estriol. These last two are bio-identical but are almost inactive and cause some health issues.

✪ Hormone replacement therapy (HRT) sometimes refers to treatment with bio-identicals and sometimes to treatment with the counterfeits!

~

PATENT, GENERIC, AND COMPOUNDED DRUGS:
When a patent is granted, the drugmakers get a twenty-year monopoly. This allows them to charge shocking prices, espe-

cially when insurance pays and the claim is made that the drug is lifesaving. These are so expensive that only an insurance company writing blank checks ever buys them. Because of this, generics are now ninety (90) percent of all drugs consumed in America.

Generic manufacturing is permitted after proprietary medications go off patent. These drugs may then be given a new trademarked name by the latest manufacturer. In theory, generics are cheaper because market demand and costs determine their price instead of the monopoly. But since insurance pays for 80 percent of all US medicines, cash prices for all drugs stay relatively high. The original manufacturers also continue to sell their brand even after patents expire.

When a patient buys a generic, they will get whatever her pharmacy bought from the wholesaler. These companies scour the international market for the cheapest choices and dump them on the domestic retailers. Estradiol generics, for example, are often quite weak. And when cardiac medications are improper, illness or even death can result. These issues are common.

US hormone physicians who figure all this out usually prefer compounders. These pharmacies manufacture medication for individual patients and are forbidden to manufacture in bulk. They must use the chemical name rather than a brand. Compounders have only their reputation for quality and service to compete against the full manufacturing and advertising might of the patent and generic drugmakers. The compound market is only a few percent of all drug sales, but if they were allowed to make whatever they wanted, medications would be far more affordable.

The Hormone Feel-Good Story is next. If you would rather read first about how the corporations have distorted hormone care, skip that and go straight to the following section, Hormones are Vilified.

Review:

✪ Provera is a trademark for synthetic methyl progesterone. It is a "progestin" or "progestogen." The natural progesterones are available from compounders as micronized capsules, dissolvable "troches," and in certain doses as patented drugs or generics. Prometrium is one brand.

✪ The estrogens: Bio-identical estradiol is available as generics, compounded drugs, and patented versions. All have chemical names and sometimes copyrighted brands. There are creams, pills, suppositories, and proprietary patches. The horse estrogen trade names include Premarin and Ogen. Their patents have expired, but the names are still copyrighted. Other generic and patented estradiol versions, sometimes with other trade names, can be found on foreign websites and with travel outside the US.

PART II
THE HORMONE FEEL-GOOD STORY

CHAPTER 3
HORMONE THERAPY FOR WOMEN

Ideal hormone levels look like this.

Menopause information is everywhere—some good, some bad, and all of it confusing. Many authorities call this unpleasant syndrome "natural" and recommend ignoring it. But hormones greatly improve women's health and menopause symptoms.

June is 49: She started estradiol, progesterone, and testosterone eight weeks ago: *Hey, doing well on my hormones. About two months in now. My energy is up, as is my sex drive and my enjoyment of it. My muscle tone and skin look great, and some old*

friends I gathered with on the East coast last week accused me of having an aging painting of myself in a closet somewhere. I'm still having hot flashes at night and wonder if I should adjust my estrogen up some? My reply was: *Increase your estradiol to two mg each morning. We may decide to increase your progesterone and will check your levels on your next office visit.*

How the female reproductive system works: Young women start with hundreds of ova or eggs. Each cycle, the uterus is prepared for a potential baby and one ovum is used. As women mature, usually in their mid-40s, the eggs run low and periods become irregular. After the eggs are gone, the cycles stop but some hormone production persists as long as the ovaries are not cut out.

This is the "change of life." Progesterone levels typically fall and estrogen production continues. Some women get depression, anxiety, irritability, and sleep disturbance. Other symptoms include bloating, acne, breast tenderness, and heavy, irregular menstrual periods.

At about age 50, women "fall off a hormonal cliff." As all their hormones decline, full menopause develops. Many are miserable and have intense hot flashes. After a few last irregular periods, they are in complete menopause, defined as a year without a menstrual cycle. Their symptoms are usually more dramatic and unpleasant than men's at the same age and often more severe than any pre-menstrual syndrome (PMS) they had earlier in their lives.

For the first several years, most women need only progesterone. As menstrual periods slow and stop, estrogen and the other hormones should be added. Estradiol has the strongest effect on hot flashes. Testosterone improves strength, alertness, sexuality, and helps with bladder and vaginal symptoms. Since it transforms into estrogen, it protects the heart in both sexes.

Patients who want simplicity or are on a tight budget sometimes use it as the sole therapy.

> **Janice, 64,** watched her husband die of lung cancer two years ago after a three-year illness and has been "out of gas" ever since. She said she was "done with men," so she flew to Los Angeles to have her breast implants taken out. Because Janice had fatigue, depression, anxiety, and no interest in sex, I discussed menopause therapy with her. She agreed to try. So I wrote a prescription for estradiol and progesterone and placed a testosterone pellet. Janice called four months later—she had a new boyfriend and felt great. She is returning to have her implants replaced.

Hormone supplementation slows and may prevent:
✪ Alzheimer's disease (AD).
✪ Heart disease.
✪ Fatigue, depression, sleep disturbance, anxiety, and irritability.
✪ Bone loss, osteoporosis, and increased chance of fractures.
✪ Skin problems including thinning, wrinkling, itching, sagging, easy injury, and loss of elasticity.
✪ Thinning of joint cartilage. Tooth loss and gum disease.
✪ Vaginal area difficulties: dry, thin, and inelastic.
✪ Spontaneous urination during coughing or lifting.
✪ Sexual decline including painful sex.

> **Linda** is a 63-year-old registered nurse: *Testosterone makes me feel sexy and gives me an overall feeling of well-being. My strength and muscle tone improve, especially when I exercise. When I was younger, I got a little aggressive when I used it, but now I am either OK with aggression, or maybe it does not happen. I have paranoia and anxiety when I do not take progesterone, even though I'm not an anxious person.*

I sometimes get a little depressed, and extra progesterone helps this. I take from one to three of the 200 mg capsules a day, and it mellows me out. With estradiol, my ability to remember improves and I sleep better. I'm less tired. I've tried different doses, and I know what works best for me.

Many women have prodigious emotional strength. They continue to function well and look attractive despite severe symptoms. It shocks my wife and me when our questionnaire reveals how miserable they are. Many admit that they feel as if the entire world is against them. Others say they are hanging on by their fingernails. Some give up and stop trying.

Many women are convinced their angst is situational or even existential rather than simply because of hormonal deficiency. They are wrong—progesterone, estradiol, and testosterone improve or cure these symptoms. Many women get complete relief using testosterone alone. DHEA, vitamin D, and melatonin are also often helpful.

Do not read this paragraph if you are politically correct. Women who have been keeping up often think they know more than I do about hormones. So I ask my patients if they are interested in feeling better and leave it at that. I never try to persuade anyone to start therapy, because leading this horse to water is all I can do. Arguing with them about whether they are thirsty is like arguing with Germans—you just piss everyone off. (Since I am German, I get a pass on this.)

Janice, 51 years old: *My marriage was disintegrating, I hated everyone around me, and I felt terrible. But I got on the hormones and they saved me. I am trying to repair all the damage I did.*

Women are the precious glue holding families together. Their proper functioning and positive feelings are everyone's bedrock. My wife Judy Yoho believes that menopause is the most common cause of divorce for couples over 45 years old and that

this therapy saves many marriages. She developed this opinion while interviewing thousands of women in our practice.

Young women who have total hysterectomies, which include ovary removal, crash into violent hormonal withdrawal and have severe hot flashes. Sexual interest declines or vanishes. The risks of stroke, fracture, heart disease, memory loss, eye deterioration, and even death increase. Immediate replacement is critical. Their situation differs from ordinary menopause, where the ovaries are intact and still partly functioning.

> **Patsy** is a 45-year-old accountant: *I had my hysterectomy* [with ovary removal] *ten years ago when my daughter was only six years old. I didn't get on hormone replacement until last year. I thought about my life and wrote my daughter an apology letter about the way I treated her. I was just so depressed and anxious. Progesterone has been the biggest relief. I feel human again.*

Cutting out the ovaries and uterus together pays better and is an easier procedure for the surgeon than only removing the uterus. Doctors sell them to patients with remarks like, "You will no longer have to worry about cancer if we cut your ovaries out." My wife and I fell for this line. But when a young woman has her ovaries removed, the premature menopause symptoms are horrific, and the risks of medical problems including heart disease increase dramatically. Ovarian cancer is a terrible disease, but it is so rare that allowing a gynecologist to castrate you to prevent it makes no sense.

Women who use estrogen get less Alzheimer's disease, and some studies say it is 80 percent preventive. But this robust scientific support is unknown to the mainstream. The current standard is to wait until after the disease has advanced, then use toxic, heavily promoted, fantastically expensive patent drugs. Even the academics who are paid to study these understand they are dubious.

AD is tragic and epidemic. Eleven percent of those over 65 have it, and it kills more people than breast and prostate cancer combined. Sixty-seven percent of Medicare long-term care payments are related to Alzheimer's, more than $250 billion a year—it is the most expensive disease in US healthcare. Our patients are being criminally mistreated.

A similar literature underpins the beneficial effects of growth hormone and testosterone for Alzheimer's and other diseases of the aging brain for both sexes.

Appendix C has over 50 citations supporting all this. Stop here and spend two minutes scanning them. If you understand this story, the rest of the book will be transparent and credible. Properly referencing every hormone subject would have required dozens of books.

CHAPTER 4
ESTROGEN FOR WOMEN

E stradiol has the most dramatic effects of any hormone. Its benefits include:

✪ Helps the heart more than other hormones.

✪ Decreases the risks of cataracts, vaginal atrophy, and macular degeneration of the retina.

✪ Reduces the chances of stroke, diabetes, colon cancer, Alzheimer's, memory problems, and osteoporosis.

✪ Cures hot flashes and improves sexuality.

From the Los Angeles Times, 1999: *I could live without my husband, children, or cats. But I could never live without my beloved estrogen.*

Who should use estrogen and how much? Menopausal women and sometimes men transitioning to women are prescribed estrogen. Men with prostate cancer are also occasionally treated with it. Women in menopause should start at 1.5 milligrams in the morning, then increase to 2 to 2.5 milligrams. This brings blood levels up to about 70 pg/ml, which protects

the heart and other organs. We believe this is safe because young, healthy women have estrogen levels in the hundreds during parts of their cycle.

Premarin, the horse estrogen, was the first treatment for menopause. It has many beneficial effects, but it causes a slight increase in blood clotting. This makes it obsolete for long-term use. Estradiol, the primary bio-identical type, is safer. Every study on it—KEEPS, EPAT, WEST, CORA, DANISH, and ELITE (those academics love acronyms)—found no increase in blood clotting.

Although the estradiol transdermal patch may provide the best relief of hot flashes and does not cause blood clots, it does not protect against heart disease. In contrast, both types of oral estrogen protect the heart. This was proven in many studies, including the CORA, ELITE, WEST, and DANISH.

Since many medical authorities think that oral estradiol and oral Premarin are the same things with the same risks, they often recommend using the patch if there are concerns about blood clotting. Doctors should instead prescribe brand name, generic, or compounded oral estradiol. These are safe and protect against heart disease and stroke.

Doctors are usually hesitant to prescribe oral estrogens for sick patients or those with heart risk factors such as smoking, obesity, or a family history. They use the patch for them if they recommend hormones at all. However, as I describe in the Be Careful Whom You Trust chapter, these are precisely the patients who need cardiac protection the most. In nearly every situation, their risk to reward ratio favors the oral type. We should accept the minor hazard of blood clotting to protect their hearts. Dr. Rouzier describes these issues in a well-referenced article.

Surgeons and anesthesiologists have many responsibilities, and they rarely read the confusing estrogen studies closely. Since blood clots after surgery are such a hazard, most of them tell

their patients to stop all replacement before surgery. Some gynecologists are adamant about this.

**Estradiol is available as generic, compounded, or patented
varieties.** Hormone doctors mostly recommend a compounding
pharmacy's product because generics are less predictable and
the patent type is too expensive if not paid for by insurance.
Brand names from foreign sources made by major manufacturers are often affordable and of excellent quality.

Estradiol patches such as Vivelle Dot (twice a week) or
Climara (once a week) may relieve menopause symptoms better
than the oral forms. The higher dose of .1 mg a day works best.
To help the transdermal patch stick, patients scrub the area with
alcohol before they apply it. The device sometimes causes skin
irritation. Some women overlap the patch with the next one by a
few days. Others use more of these than the manufacturer
recommends. Both are healthy practices that deliver higher
estrogen levels.

The Femring vaginal insert, which looks like a diaphragm
without a cap over the ring, is marketed as hormone replacement and produces good blood levels. The higher dose of 1 mg
of estradiol per day works best. It stays in place for two to three
months, then is replaced.

Some patients take oral estradiol but still have persistent
vaginal dryness. Estrogen vaginal cream helps, but as the only
source of estrogen, it is not usually enough. Compounded
dissolvable vaginal tablets called "troches" supply more. The
typical dose is half of a .05 mg tablet. Special applicators make
insertion easy. Patients use one a night for the first seven days,
then a few times a week. A patented type is available, but the
dose is too low to affect the entire body.

Estring looks like the Femring. Vaginal symptoms are
relieved, but it is not designed to produce enough estrogen for
the entire body.

Suzanne Somers popularized two other bio-identical estro-

gens, estrone, and estriol. These are only $1/80^{th}$ as active as estradiol. Estriol's effects are primarily on the vagina, and it causes general swelling. It may have some unique benefits, however. Estrone has been associated with breast cancer. Compounding pharmacies and doctors sometimes market combinations of these three natural estrogens, but this is a useless expense because the body manufactures the other two from estradiol.

Each woman needs to find what works best for her. Physicians should allow patients to experiment with their doses within guidelines. Most women feel best when they have high estrogen blood levels, and this also gives them the best disease protection.

CHAPTER 5

PROGESTERONE AND TESTOSTERONE FOR WOMEN

PROGESTERONE in proper doses helps sleep, hot flashes, depression, anxiety, irritability, migraine headaches, and decreases breast and nipple tenderness because of estrogen. There is evidence that it lowers the risks of heart disease, reduces the chances of breast and ovarian cancer, and might be of benefit treating breast cancer. Substantial laboratory science shows that progesterone suppresses ovarian cancer.

Stella is an entrepreneur and co-founder of a start-up medical company. She said: *I'm 47 years old and have felt terrible for several years. I'm angry, irritable, and tough on everyone around me. In my defense, I am working 65 to 70 hours a week. My doctor finally increased my progesterone to eight of the 200 mg capsules a day. They are my pacifiers. Even when I took six of them, I was still impossible to be around. I've tried antidepressants and tranquilizers, but nothing else worked. My husband was very patient with me for years and put up with a lot. He never used the "B" word, but that was what I was. I'm still not a super-agreeable person, but this has been the difference between being functional and being antisocial.*

How progesterone is taken: Any time estrogen is used for menopause, true progesterone should be prescribed almost automatically. This decreases the chances of uterine cancer to less than the risk for woman who take no hormones. Even after a hysterectomy, progesterone should still be taken because of its many benefits. High enough doses should be given to relieve depression, insomnia, and anxiety. This ranges from 100 to 800 mg a day or more.

Modern progesterone and other hormones can be "micronized," which means spread over many tiny particles. This creates a slow-release type that can be taken orally. These cause sleepiness and are usually taken at bedtime. Progesterone troches are another formulation that dissolve in the mouth but may be less well-absorbed. The rapidly dissolving type (RDT) may taste the best. These occasionally cause nausea, but using them in the rectum or vagina does not. Since they do not cause sleepiness, patients can take troches during the day.

> **Julie** is 38 years old. *I had miserable PMS for two weeks before each of my periods. The only time I felt really normal was when I was pregnant.* [Author's note: progesterone levels during pregnancy are sky high.] *But since I've been using progesterone during the second half of my cycle, I've felt great all the time.*

Treating premenstrual syndrome (PMS) with progesterone: Many young women have depression, anxiety, and irritability for the three to 14 days before their menstrual periods when progesterone is lowest. This may be effectively treated with progesterone. Depending on how the patient responds, one to eight of the 200 mg capsules or troches are used each day while the symptoms are active.

A mother's progesterone blood levels are several hundred ng/ml just before she delivers a baby. After delivery, these crash, and some get a severe "postpartum" depression. Most doctors prescribe antidepressants, even though high-dose progesterone is far safer and more effective. One hundred mg of progesterone in oil given intra-muscularly makes these women feel normal within an hour. Alternatively, they might take a 200 mg oral capsule or troche every hour until symptoms improve. Doses of 1600 mg are safe. We know it is reasonable because these patients had similar levels during their entire pregnancy.

> **Fran** is 63 years old: *I have been on Prozac for 20 years, up to 80 mg a day. I stopped it after you started me on bio-identical hormones and especially progesterone. With 800 mg at bedtime, I get the best sleep of the past 20 years and am no longer anxious and depressed.* Note: This is unusual. Most people who have taken an SSRI antidepressant like Prozac for years are stuck on them. They are addictive, and the withdrawal symptoms mimic the depression and anxiety they are claimed to treat. Instead of Prozac, Fran now takes four progesterone capsules. Although this seems like a high dose, it is harmless for women.

Provera, the brand-name imitation progesterone, is now off-patent. It makes many women feel lousy and slightly increases their chance of getting breast cancer. It should never be used long-term for menopause, but it is still valuable to treat vaginal bleeding. A longer-acting injection is used for birth control, but this causes consistent weight gain, heart disease, and has been found to double the risk of breast cancer. It also has a withdrawal syndrome of fatigue, dry heaves, nausea, and breast tenderness. Although the contraceptive use of Provera should be banned, some doctors ignore these problems and retail it in their offices, anyway.

Prometrium is a branded bio-identical oral progesterone that has been patented for the 100 and 200 mg dose. Strangely, it has the same warnings on its label as Provera. The manufacturer must have copied the Provera disclaimers, assuming the side

effects were the same. This is wrong—every type of real progesterone is entirely safe for women.

For men transitioning to women, the Endocrine Society
recommends both progesterone and estrogen. But progesterone
causes inflammatory heart disease and other health issues in
genetic men. Estrogen does not.

TESTOSTERONE IS SAFE, AND EVEN WHEN USED ALONE TREATS
most menopause symptoms and promotes gradual weight loss.
Diabetes improves, and migraine headaches often vanish.
Testosterone decreases the chance of heart disease for both men
and women. Breast cancer rates decline 70 percent according to
a study of patients using subcutaneous pellets.

> **Samantha's** text message: *Good morning Dr, I'm 47 will be 48 this
> year. Now about menopause, I actually have a few symptoms, but I
> don't really know. I get a birth Control shot every three months, and
> it stops my menstrual cycle so I actually have not had a period for
> around five years so as for menopause it's up in the air LOL. OK, so
> now about this shot you gave me (she received a testosterone pellet). I
> believe it's going on for three months. It took a couple of weeks for it
> to kick in, but immediately when it did, I knew something was
> different, had lots of energy, and I felt totally different. I was reading
> the article you sent me—a couple there mentioned having felt young
> again, and I have to say that is absolutely very true. It all came
> together, everything it said on there, that's exactly how I was feeling.
> I felt young, energetic with a sex drive which I have not had in about
> two years being with my husband almost going on 30 years love him
> to death but sad to say since about a year and a half ago I try to avoid
> sex at all costs even sleeping on the couch which kind of sucks for him
> but, of course, I always gave it to him. But a month after I got this
> shot everything changed completely now it actually feels fun again*

like I said it's no longer a chore lol to be honest when you told me about this in the office I did not believe you, but now I don't think I could be without this shot it feels good to feel young again please let me know when you're back in the office LOL till then I will be using the cream hopefully it has the same effect ty. I don't want this feeling to go away pol I actually lost some weight without even trying, and I have a lot of energy I actually love my husband again LOL just kidding I always loved him but sexually it was more of a chore for me, and now I'm actually enjoying it again. Have a blessed day. She lives far from my office, so I prescribed a higher dose of testosterone cream to replace the three-month testosterone pellet.

Women have ten times more testosterone than estrogen in their bodies, and men have far more than this. The numbers are confusing because the units are different. In both sexes, testosterone also supplies estrogen with a conversion process.

Testosterone supplementation has few side effects except occasional hair growth and acne. The acne may be treated by decreasing the dose or by prescribing spironolactone, a weak diuretic with anti-inflammatory properties (doses range from 50 mg a day to 100 mg twice a day). Some women view testosterone-induced sexual interest as a side effect, especially if they do not feel close to their husband or partner.

Julie is 59 years old: *Nothing I did helped my weight until I tried testosterone pellets, but once I got on them, I lost 25 pounds over nine months and felt fantastic. I thought I was cured and didn't go back to you for five months and gained back ten pounds. When I returned, you put in another pellet and prescribed testosterone cream to use if I couldn't make it into the office.*

How testosterone is used: Cream testosterone can be applied every other day or even twice a week for women. This usually produces adequate blood levels and symptom relief. Application to the vagina, inner thighs, or arms works well. Although other doctors may prescribe less, I start with a half cc of 20-50 mg/cc cream every other day. I instruct patients to increase or decrease this dose depending on how they feel, then let me know what happens. Other women may get enough testosterone through skin-to-skin contact with a partner who is using a stronger type.

Testosterone pellets were developed in 1942. They make some women feel even better than the creams or injections. Insertion is painless, and the pellets for women from the Anazao compounding pharmacy last 2 1/2 to 3 months. (Robert L. Morgan, NP: *The compounder we use, Belmar in Colorado, makes pellets that last 5-6 months.*) Women need a milligram per pound, 1/10th of the male dose. For example, two of the 100 mg rice-sized pellets are the dose for a 200-pound woman.

I call some of my patients "pellet Superwomen." They look great and feel better.

This is what one of them says.

To insert pellets, I clean the skin with chlorhexidine scrub and inject a local anesthetic. Then, I use a hollow needle to insert the dissolvable drug into fat through the inside of the belly button. This does not produce a visible scar.

This video shows the insertion process.

Injectable testosterone for women requires only a tiny volume: 1/10 to 2/10 cc (20 to 40 mg of testosterone cypionate or enanthate, 200 mg/cc). Shots like this can be done using a thin needle. They are not painful and are placed into fat rather than muscle anywhere on the body.

Some senior women dislike applying creams. Although oral testosterone is not strong enough for most women, it works well enough for them because they may need less than younger women. This can be compounded into micronized 25 to 100 mg capsules. The dose is adjusted as needed for symptom relief. Some women in this age group regard sexual effects as undesirable, but since they only receive a small amount, this is not much of a problem.

Are you are going to a desert island? If you could take only one hormone, take testosterone.

CHAPTER 6

TESTOSTERONE FOR MEN

Men need testosterone. The benefits are enormous and the risks almost nonexistent. To learn how the bad press was contrived, read the Killing Testosterone With Fake News chapter later.

Steven is an 82-year-old retired CEO of a major media company: *I had lost all strength, and I was sitting in a wheelchair in a Palm Springs nursing home. The staff had to lift me in and out of bed. I was inches from being snuffed out. Then my doctor started coming in every week and giving me testosterone shots. In six weeks, I stood up and walked out of there, back into my life.* (Note: this can also work for women.)

Men's symptoms: Starting around thirty years old, testosterone blood levels fall about a percent a year. Muscular strength, sexuality, and energy levels slowly decrease. Recovery from exercise gets slower, and some men notice reduced intellectual capabilities. Bone density falls, but fractures are less common in men than women since men start higher. Atrial fibrillation and stroke are more common with low testosterone levels. Skin problems, heart disease, hot flashes, dental issues, and irritability increase as testosterone declines. Some of these disorders must be treated early or they are irreversible.

> **Sam** is a beloved 83-year-old physician: *I was about to give up. I just had a knee replacement, and I have osteoporosis. The author sent me some cream testosterone as a gift, and now I think I'm going to live fifteen more years! I can't thank him enough, and I'm indebted to him forever for his kindness. I'm doing well, much better than I ever expected.*

Testosterone has many benefits. Using it gradually improves health over at least a decade. Testosterone supplementation has the following effects:

✪ Strength increases, cholesterol falls, and weight loss is progressive.

✪ Sexuality improves—morning erections return, for example.

✪ Heart disease risks decline.

✪ Diabetes and migraine headaches get better and are sometimes cured.

✪ Testosterone supplementation decreases anxiety and improves mood.

Testosterone levels also relate to health:

✪ Older men with higher testosterone levels had better results on intellectual testing.

✪ Lower levels were associated with earlier death in men. They correlated also with coronary disease.

Testosterone transforms into estrogen in both men and women. This "female" hormone helps sexuality in either sex and protects the heart better than any other hormone. Sometimes estrogen blood levels do not rise to those of younger men even with aggressive testosterone supplementation. So a few physicians are starting to prescribe estradiol for men. This will vastly improve cholesterol numbers.

Testosterone has a few side effects. Hair loss and hair growth can happen but are of no consequence compared to the benefits. Acne is rarely a significant problem but may be treated with traditional medications such as Retin-A.

Testosterone often makes testicles (balls) shrink, and this may be permanent. Sleep apnea, which is obstructed breathing while asleep, has been reported. The studies describing this are weak.

Some bodybuilders use doses that are ten times those for seniors (imagine injecting yourself with 10 cc of testosterone oil each week, ouch). Some of them also use anabolic steroids, which are testosterone relatives that have related effects. Taking all these drugs can decrease "good" cholesterol (high-density lipoprotein, HDL) and thus may be a risk for coronary artery disease. The smaller doses prescribed for older people usually improve cholesterol numbers, however. Cream testosterone rarely lowers HDL the way the injectables sometimes do.

Men who use testosterone for five years or more have reduced sperm counts and are often sterile. Because of this, the drug has been evaluated as a male contraception. In one study, Chinese men were given injections of testosterone undecanoate, a long-acting type of natural testosterone. One percent of them conceived after 30 months. This is more effective than condoms but not as effective as birth control pills for women. In a second study of 399 men and a third trial of 271, weekly testosterone enanthate shots lowered most of their sperm counts and produced consistent infertility. It was reversible after the treatment was stopped. A few of the men's sperm counts never decreased, possibly because injections were missed. There were a few pregnancies.

Two drugs raise testosterone by stimulating its natural production. These are clomiphene (Clomid), a 25-50 mg daily pill, and human chorionic gonadotrophin (HCG), an injection given several times a week. These may be prescribed to raise testosterone levels for younger men who need to preserve their fertility. But beyond 40 to 50 years of age, men who take therapeutic doses of testosterone may become permanently sterile.

Patients who are in treatment or evaluation for prostate cancer are traditionally advised to avoid testosterone. For a complete explanation of this issue, see the Killing Testosterone with Fake News and The Prostate Cancer Meat Grinder section of Butchered by "Healthcare" in the bonus section.

> **John** is a 61-year-old physician: *I was on cream testosterone for over a decade and must have had excellent results. But when I started injecting testosterone cypionate once a week, I noticed an improvement. Not only was I more muscular, but I started having sex with my wife about every 36 hours. She was on testosterone too, so it was great.*

Testosterone is given in creams, injections, or pellets. Atriva and versa creams can be mixed with testosterone to aid absorption through the skin. This can be formulated in 100 to 200 mg/gram strengths for men, which is 10-20 percent. Rubbing one to two cc into the skin of the inner thigh or arm twice a day elevates blood levels properly. Using the cream on the thinner skin of the scrotum may produce better absorption, so patients need less.

Testosterone cream may be accidentally transferred to others through close personal contact. Sex, skin-to-skin touching, and bedsheet exposures can do this. This could be an annoyance or occasionally it is a disaster. Women who receive large doses may develop acne, hair growth, a deeper voice, and an enlarged clitoris. Children who are exposed can have early sexual development and a short final height. If pregnant women take or unwittingly receive testosterone, their fetuses may develop congenital disabilities. Babies of nursing mothers sometimes have other injuries.

After applying testosterone cream, we instruct our male patients to wait 4 hours before skin contact with anyone else. Transfer of cream from women to men is of little consequence because testosterone cream for women is so much weaker than a man's.

The Androderm testosterone patch is weak, expensive, and a hassle. Androgel is a low strength as well, 1 or 1.62 percent. This produces blood levels of only 500-600 ng/dl. Compare these patented products with compounded cream: 10 or 20 percent compound testosterone often provides more desirable blood levels of 1000-1500 ng/dl. Levels such as these build strength, vitality, and improve cholesterol numbers the most. Still higher levels (over 2000) may not improve function and might even decrease sexual interest. Each patient's therapy must be individualized for best results.

Testosterone cypionate or enanthate shots (both 200 mg/cc and nearly the same thing) are cheap and convenient. Some physicians mix one of these intermediate-acting testosterones with a short-acting one, propionate. One cc a week of the combination is the usual dose. Undecanoate is another natural testosterone that only requires injection once every three months (available in most of the developed world but not the US).

Injection into either fat or muscle works, but injection of the male-type doses into fat produces more soreness and bruising. For women, the volume is so small that it makes little difference. After each shot, blood levels elevate, then fall. Biological testosterone production is even and steady, so some people try to mimic this by injecting a half cc twice a week. Some even divide the doses into daily injections of .15 cc. Creams produce more stable blood levels, so they might work best.

Pellets require a brief surgical procedure using a local anesthetic to implant them into the fat under the skin. These produce steady levels that stay high for about five months in men. The dose is ten milligrams per pound, which means a 200-pound man needs ten 200 mg pellets. These are larger than the ones used for women. Blood levels may not go above 1000 ng/dl, and some patients have a sore spot for a month. Infections or allergic reactions at the injection site are rare, but they occasionally happen. My opinion is that using one or two small pellets for women works well, but that the larger dose needed for men is too much hassle for most.

CHAPTER 7
HORMONES FOR BOTH SEXES

W hich replacements do men and women sense the most? Many women feel distinct improvements when they use thyroid, estrogen, testosterone, or progesterone. Some have dramatic responses to vitamin D. For men, testosterone is the most noticeable and some feel better with HGH. A few older men improve when they only take DHEA.

See Appendix A and B for dosing and blood testing information about each hormone.

Sally's story: *I started menopausal symptoms at 29. I was not a healthy individual. It took coming to you, and you asked how I felt. You actually let me adjust the dosage and fine-tune myself, and now I feel attractive and I'm sleeping again. It's just a better overall quality of life that I didn't have for eleven years. I would go to doctors and they would say my hormones were in the normal range, but I didn't feel good... They didn't give me enough... I felt amazing within two to four weeks after I started...*

Another story.

MELATONIN is a harmless but potent antioxidant or clean-up hormone with many benefits. It is taken at bedtime and improves sleep. It also helps mood, migraines, energy, and the immune system. Dentists say that patients taking melatonin have improved gum and mouth health. It has favorable effects on both breast and prostate cancer.

Some use it to reset the sleep-wake cycle. When travelers enter a new time zone, they take up to 100 mg on the first night. Melatonin has also been used to help addicts stop Valium and related sedatives. And it decreases nighttime urination for men with large prostates.

An anecdote: Those taking melatonin may see their grey or white hair gradually change back to the original color. As this happens, they get dark roots and white tips, which is the reverse of what happens to dyed hair as it grows out. This may mean their health is getting better.

The best melatonin preparations last six hours or longer. Compounders make these slow-release products as prescriptions. These are also available over-the-counter for purchase at either Nutrascriptives.com or LifeExtension.com. The melatonin capsules made by compounders are 1, 2, 3, and 5 milligrams and higher. Women start at 1 mg and men at 3 mg. Dosage is increased until good sleep or side effects occur. For men, the average dose needed is 9 to 30 mg and for women, 1 to 30 mg.

Up to 100 mg every night is safe and some people need that much.

The only problems with melatonin are sleepiness and vivid dreams. Since it is taken at bedtime, most people do not mind these, although a few become agitated and cannot tolerate it. Several weeks may go by before the full response occurs. Some people must take melatonin several hours before going to bed because it has a slow onset for them. These effects are individual.

I wanted to have dark hair, but melatonin gave me restless sleep. So I am still using dye.

VITAMIN D (D3) IS A STEROID HORMONE, JUST LIKE ESTROGEN OR testosterone. True vitamins cannot be made by the body, but this is produced in the skin during sun exposure. Those with a deficiency who take it often get an energy boost and have less joint pain.

> **Susan** is 63 years old and has a vitamin D level of only 11 ng/ml. She is black, vegan, has high blood pressure, and gets little sun exposure. She wears sunscreen every day and takes Norvasc, a high blood pressure medicine. These all make D deficiency more likely. Susan would probably feel more energetic if she took supplements and had higher levels.

A 2015 Danish study tested 247,000 patients and found their average health was better if their D3 levels were 60-100 ng/ml. This is much higher than the traditional goal of 30 ng/ml. In the people with higher numbers, there were fewer strokes and less heart disease. They had reduced rates of dementia, obesity, prostate cancer, and colon cancer. The patients with lower levels had more depression, hypertension, and arthritis. Recent studies show that the people who get sick with COVID also have low levels.

Although this "observational" study suggests benefits, we do not know with certainty that *taking* vitamin D is worthwhile. Definitive evidence would require giving D3 to one group and comparing them with a similar group taking sugar pills. If the health of the ones using D improved, it would prove that the hormone works. But RCTs are seldom done with medications like Vitamin D or other bio-identicals because they cannot be patented to make the huge profits.

At least half of us have D3 levels below 60. This vitamin is cheap, over-the-counter, and almost harmless in the usual doses, so taking it seems reasonable. If the advantages of supplementation are borne out in further study, the medical mainstream would agree. But D is generic and inexpensive. The industry has no incentive to examine it.

Human skin manufactures vitamin D during sun exposure. But nearly equatorial conditions are necessary to produce high levels. Also, seniors lose their ability to produce enough D, even when they live in Palm Springs and their skin looks like an alligator's. And our dermatologists have us wearing sunscreen and hats to prevent skin cancer. This must have lowered average D levels as well.

Vitamin D (D3) comes in 2,000, 5,000 and 10,000 international unit (IU) capsules. A conservative place to start is 5000 IU a day if you are under 200 pounds and 10,000 IU if you are heavier. But many people need 15,000 or more to bring their blood levels close to 100 ng/ml. My energy improves when my levels get this high. Note: D3 is over-the-counter and derived from animals. *D2* is a prescription that is made from plants. It has been studied in the treatment of rickets and other medical conditions and is weaker than D3.

There are anecdotes about D's healing effects on joints and other systems when blood levels are 130 or higher. Although

Florida lifeguards have numbers like this from the sun, in most circumstances this only happens when large doses are taken. If you decide to use more D, read about it and take responsibility —I am not formally recommending it. Check your blood levels through your doctor or with the Life Extension website. They will have your blood drawn at a national lab near your home and email you the results. Over-the-counter home testing kits are less accurate.

Some references make vitamin D sound like a cure-all, but panaceas are mythical. As long as you watch your levels, taking somewhat higher than the usual doses may be no more dangerous than working as a lifeguard. Like other medical fields, we know less than we claim about D.

DHEA FUNCTIONS LIKE A MILD TESTOSTERONE IN A PILL. IT energizes, enhances mood, decreases joint pain, and reduces belly fat. For some, it is an antidepressant. It maintains sexuality and improves diabetes. Death rates are lower for people taking DHEA. There is ongoing research about using it to treat both heart and Alzheimer's disease. A bio-identical DHEA called Prastera is patented for 200 mg and FDA approved for systemic lupus, a severe inflammatory disease.

> **Alex**, 71 years old: *I tried testosterone recently, but it gave me trouble urinating. DHEA makes me feel stronger and more energetic without this side effect.*

DHEA has no serious side effects. Doses vary between 10 and 200 mg. Older patients are less sensitive, and many feel no improvement with it. Younger women sometimes get acne or hair growth when they take only 20 mg a day. The acne can be treated with dose reduction or spironolactone, 50 to 100 mg twice a day.

Most over-the-counter DHEA works poorly because it only lasts about an hour in the body. The compounded slow-release micronized version is much more effective. Compounders make the long-acting versions as prescriptions and nutrascriptives.com sells it over-the-counter. The usual starting dose for men is 50 mg and for women 10 to 20 mg. It is taken in the evening.

People in their 60s and beyond may benefit from high doses of DHEA. Up to 500 to 600 milligrams a day may improve arthritis symptoms. This helps some women continue athletics into their 70s and 80s. Their blood levels are much higher than the laboratory "normals."

Intrarose is a branded DHEA vaginal insert that is patented for 6.5 mg. It has been available since 2016. I recommend a stronger version from a compounding pharmacy, however,—20 mg of DHEA combined with 1 mg of estradiol. Women who use this say that painful sex becomes a thing of the past.

HUMAN GROWTH HORMONE (HGH) CAN PRODUCE A burst of energy, but some patients may not feel it for six months, and some never do. It reduces fat and improves other measures of health. And it is a potential cure for osteoporosis since HGH can increase bone density five percent a year. Diabetes gets better and sometimes goes away. Muscle strength normalizes. The hormone prevents most Alzheimer's disease (Appendix C).

> **Jack** is 66 years old, a respected real estate entrepreneur, and a lifelong weightlifting enthusiast. For the past seven years, his elbows have been too sore for him to lift much. He told me they were "done." But when Jack started using testosterone along

with 200 mg a day of long-acting DHEA, the soreness went away. He said, "The guns are coming back." Then he started HGH. Two months later, he was lifting weights four days a week. He told me, "my elbows stopped talking to me."

As we age, our eye lenses harden and we lose the ability to focus. But some patients in their late 50s taking HGH can still see clearly up close and also at a distance. Their lens elasticity has been preserved and sometimes improves. Ophthalmologists have confirmed this by examining these people at intervals during HGH therapy.

HGH is a prescription given by daily injection that can cost $1000 a month or more. Over-the-counter oral "supplements" are not to be trusted.

See the Growth Hormone Was Smeared chapter for more.

Robert is a 58-year-old attorney: *I went to my doctor to have a hernia repair. He sent me for an exercise test, which was positive. I then had a coronary angiogram that showed blockages of my heart arteries. The docs wanted to do stents and maybe heart surgery before my hernia surgery, but I said no way, I felt fine. So I saw a doctor. After a year on hormones, including HGH, I returned to that cardiologist, and my arteries were clear. They let me have my hernia surgery, but none of the docs believed the treatment cured my coronary arteries.* Author's note: I heard this story secondhand.

THYROID is the master and commander of the hormone ship. It is so important that I have an entire section about it later.

PART III
HORMONES ARE VILIFIED

CHAPTER 8
HOW HORMONE USAGE WAS SUPPRESSED

Cui Bono, the Latin phrase meaning "who benefits," says the motive for an act or crime lies with the person who has something to gain.

Only twenty percent of our senior women and even fewer men take hormones. Outside Europe and the US, usage is rare. How is this possible? The "bio-identical" or "human" forms of these drugs are not promoted because they can rarely be patented to make the big money. But they work better and are safer than other medications such as statins, antidepressants, many cancer treatments, and the proprietary imitation hormones made by big Pharma. These industry cash cows are supported and protected, while in contrast, natural hormones are defamed and restricted. Chasing profits has ruined science.

To explain, here is how the Women's Health Initiative study (WHI) was hijacked by its own authors and sabotaged patient care. This huge National Institutes of Health trial (published in 2002) examined 160,000 women aged 59 to 79. It found an increase in breast cancer for patients taking both Premarin, the horse urine estrogen, and Provera, the patented synthetic progesterone. But those who took only Premarin had a *decrease* in breast cancer. This proved Provera was responsible, and other trials confirmed it. The WHI should have ended this medication's use for long-term applications, but it did not.

The WHI took 11 years, and by that time it was complete, the two drugs it examined were obsolete. But the study statisticians claimed they uncovered critical dangers, and the authors sensationalized and embellished their threadbare findings. Medical academics buffed their reputations by declaring that they, too, could see the emperor's clothes. The media joined the parade—baloney sells advertising—and the public soon believed that all female hormones were killers. This "man bites dog" story still terrifies everyone. Once a bell is rung, it cannot be unrung.

In the public and medical eye, hormones were branded with cancer, dementia, and other problems. One reviewer wrote that the study authors were "overselling hysteria." John Goldman, MD, wrote in Medscape, "[The study] has undermined the credibility of the research and the medical community as a whole." Abraham Morgentaler, MD, and others (Harvard) explained how the panic was generated:

> The (WHI)... *reported increased risk of adverse events of only 19 events per 10,000 person-years of exposure for the estrogen– progesterone arm* [Premarin-Provera] *compared with placebo. This means that if one woman in every generation of a family used estrogen–progesterone for 10 years, it would take 50 generations, or about 1,000 years, to see one extra adverse event in that family. The result may have been statistically significant, but they were clinically meaningless.*

Avrum Bluming and Carol Tavris described the study's statistical trickery and atrocious sensationalism in *Estrogen Matters* (2018), a superb book about the science and politics. One of the WHI's principal investigators, Rossouw, had an agenda to "change the thinking about hormones." Six years before the WHI was published, he wrote it was time to put "the brakes on that bandwagon," referring to the growing support for estrogen replacement. And so the WHI authors ignored their colleagues' advice and rushed to publication before completing the study. This spawned thousands of meritless lawsuits.

Bluming and Tavris cited follow up trials showing that estrogen decreases the chance of breast cancer, heart disease, colon cancer, osteoporosis, and ovarian cancer. Women taking it live longer on average, even the ones with breast cancer. A few studies suggested increased risks when estrogens were started ten years or more after menopause, but these numbers were insignificant compared with the enormous benefits of therapy.

The WHI, including the diet trials, cost about $1 billion— likely the most expensive research in history. Money like this buys a lot of puffery, and their deceptions still circulate. For example, the WHI ended the estrogen-only arm of the study early because the drug raised nonfatal strokes by 12 per 10,000 women per year. However, the WHI investigators included inconsequential neurologic deficits that went away in a day or two in their stroke definition. Another claim was that patients taking both Premarin and Provera had a 30 percent increase in breast cancer cases and that this decreased after the women stopped the drugs. This was true, but *it was entirely because of Provera, the outdated synthetic progesterone.* And the difference in *fatalities*—the best measure of disease—was minuscule.

At one time, Premarin and Provera were the best we had. The use of these decreases menopause symptoms and improves overall health. For example, forty (40) observational trials, mostly studying Premarin, show that estrogens reduce heart attacks by 50 percent. These are still useful short-term to control uterine bleeding, but they should never be prescribed as long-term hormone replacement.

The WHI did not evaluate estradiol or true progesterone, which have few side effects and are profoundly beneficial. Sophisticated doctors now use them almost exclusively. Soon after the WHI was published, other studies showed that these natural substances *decreased* cancer (2012 Danish trial), heart disease, and dementia (Oxford Academic), and likely even extended lifespan. Despite the availability of these alternatives, the "legal climate" created by the WHI cowed most physicians. Many refuse to take even trivial risks to help their patients. Some are afraid to prescribe hormones at all.

The WHI media frenzy lasted decades. Premarin had been the most prescribed medicine in America for many years and was still number four in 2002. But sales dropped 50 percent in the first month after the WHI came out. The most unthinkable part of the saga was that *doctors instantly forgot their 100 years of clinical experience proving that hormones were safe and effective.*

As the **WHI** lunacy infected medical thought, hormones were further maligned:

◎ **Estrogen and progesterone:** The Food and Drug Administration (FDA) smeared these with an ominous "black box" warning. (2003). It said these increased the chances of stroke, blood clots, breast cancer, and heart disease. They based these claims on the hazards of industry's own patented chemicals and not the bio-identicals.

◎ **Testosterone:** The FDA put a black box on this as well, claiming it caused heart attacks and strokes. But reviewers refuted this, saying that it enhanced heart function and *lowered* heart disease risks. An international consensus conference sponsored by the Mayo Clinic concluded that testosterone improved health, including heart disease. Other physicians debunked the

flawed testosterone studies that were cited to contrive the warning.

The FDA requires labels saying testosterone is contraindicated for men who have had prostate cancer. This is not true either, as articles in sciencedirect.com and the Journal of Urology attest.

✪ **Thyroid**: Inexpensive pork thyroid extract has been prescribed safely since the late 1800s. But the drug industry claims their synthetic T4 is superior. Pharma gives the Endocrine Society millions of dollars a year, so they recite this party line. Since T4 is missing a critical ingredient, many patients have inferior results using it compared to those who take thyroid with both T3 and T4.

✪ **Growth hormone (HGH)** was rumored to cause cancer by the FDA (2020) and others. A study of 6840 patients refuted this. Regulations made the medication hard to prescribe or possibly even illegal, and proprietary manufacturing made it phenomenally expensive. The same sports doping issues as testosterone have tarred it as well. Although the economic free-for-all impedes genuine science, our fifty years' experience suggests that it could be the safest and most effective hormone for overall health.

✪ **True progesterone** has many virtues including relieving anxiety, promoting sleep, and suppressing cancer. But its use has been thwarted with an absurd narrative. Since progesterone protects against uterine (womb) cancer, gynecologists and others had the clever insight that it is not needed for women who have had a hysterectomy. They would deny progesterone's benefits to the full third of US women over 50 who have had their uteri removed. This fatuous story somehow persuades many doctors.

✪ **Insulin**: No one could ever pretend the most indispensable medication in history was harmful. But a proprietary manufacturing process was invented, and the prices were jacked up stratospherically. Big Pharma then gifted us with several genera-

tions of progressively more expensive products with little difference between them besides marketing. While this happened,
affordable pork and beef insulin were removed from the market.
These are inferior but should stay available because some needy
patients cannot afford the latest concoctions and are rationing
their medicine. A few are dying.

WHO CARES ABOUT THE PATIENTS?

❂ **The drug manufacturers?** Remember, with few exceptions, bio-identical substances cannot be patented. This makes
them economic competitors for industry's profitable chemicals
made from dyes, coal tar, or animals.

❂ **The doctors?** Big Pharma writes their studies and standards (see The Journal's Sins chapter).

❂ **The FDA?** The Agency is now nearly a wholly-owned
subsidiary of the drugmakers because they feed it the vast
majority of its budget through "user fees." (See the FDA
chapter.)

❂ **The media?** The press says: "If a story bleeds, it leads."
Translated: their mission is to use sensationalism to sell advertising. Little integrity remains. The bulk of their stories are
extreme, negative, poorly researched, and even hysterical. An
estrogen tale without a breast cancer "hook" gets buried. They
deride testosterone as nearly an evil twin of street meth-
amphetamine, and their news about sports usage is malevolent.

CONTRARY TO ALL THIS, THE SCIENTIFIC EVIDENCE BACKING
hormone replacement is robust. Our century-long study of the
human glandular (endocrine) system taught us how hormones
function in the body, and our experience using them is enor-

mous. Thyroid has been supplemented since the late 1800s. Insulin, since 1922, and testosterone since 1935. Estrogen was developed in the 1930s and HGH in the late 1950s. *Our background with these medications is as comprehensive as any used in healthcare, and we have thousands of observational studies confirming their efficacy.*

What is happening now: Most "mainstream doctors," including endocrinologists and the rest of the internists, continue to say these benefits are modest or even unproven. They parrot the industry and FDA claims that hormones increase cancer, blood clots, and heart disease. They use inadequate doses or refuse to prescribe these medications except insulin and thyroid. Many say that hot flashes, depression, muscle wasting, and declining sexuality in older people are "healthy aging." They believe the average hormone blood levels seen in seniors are appropriate.

"Hormone doctors" have broken away from this thinking. They specialize in treating age-related hormone decline and mostly prescribe the bio-identicals. Although replacing hormone deficiencies is state-of-the-art, it is not a novel principle. It is an established, venerable idea that was first pioneered in the 1800s with porcine thyroid. Later, insulin was used, and then estrogen, testosterone, and the others.

The patients, like most doctors, were fooled by the WHI and the subsequent furor. Many women stopped their hormones. Some decided not to start and missed the critical time in early menopause when these have the most beneficial effects. This created millions more medical problems including Alzheimer's.

Doctors have a nearly religious belief that randomized controlled trials (RCTs) are the "gold standard" for medical proof. Few exist for these medications, so how can these claims be true?

Follow the money. Drugmakers seldom study natural substances because they can seldom be patented for the

monopoly advantages. In contrast, for proprietary drugs, profits are colossal, expensive trials are bargains, and there are overwhelming incentives to game the system. So "science" is designed to make the patented ones look good and discredit the bio-identicals.

Here is how RCTs are supposed to work: During a study, neither doctors nor patients are told which is the drug and which is the sugar pill. In the end, the results are "unblinded" and the patients who are taking the active substance are compared with the other group. Statistics are used to examine the results. If a medication works better and has fewer side effects, it is judged a success. The drugmaker then presents the information to the Food and Drug Administration for approval. If they grant the company a patent, the drugmaker starts "printing money" with their new medication.

For decades, with the cooperation of the FDA, the drug industry has spoiled the validity of these studies. The hoaxes they used include biased patient selection, frauds during the study, deceptive data interpretation, a rubber stamp approval process, and universal drugmaker ghostwriting for the medical journals. This has made the current RCTs garbage-in-garbage-out. By now, doctors cannot decipher what works and what is bogus. Surprisingly, only a few physicians and scientists are prosecuted out of the multitude who commit these blatant, public misdeeds. For proof of all this, see Ben Goldacre's *Bad Pharma* (2012).

Controlled trials are designed to ferret out "statistically significant" differences between placebos and active medications. Even if studies are performed without cheating—a rare event now—these differences are almost always minute. This means that—despite any claims of "statistical significance,"—the medications that were examined are useless or nearly useless. But so much money is changing hands that profitable "therapeutic breakthroughs" are publicized all the time.

For example, statin anti-cholesterol medications were FDA approved based on tiny numbers that suggested benefits. But statisticians on company payrolls cooked the figures, claimed that statins were justified for nearly everyone, and they became phenomenal best-sellers. The reality: they are marginally useful for a single-digit percent of those who take them now and a net harm for the rest. For the story of how the drugmakers trumped-up statins into today's financial colossus, see *Butchered by "Healthcare."*

Even a half-blind mathematician in a drug company's dimly lit basement understands that a RCT is unnecessary to determine whether putting a dislocated shoulder back in place works. Even a raise or a larger salary cannot motivate most researchers to deny such an obvious truth. I am wrong about some of them because they are part of the chorus denying the efficacy of hormone therapy despite the staggering evidence that proves it is beneficial.

Should we throw out everything we learned over the past century and trust the WHI media storm? I think not. Should we believe the FDA? Most of their funding comes from Pharma. Do doctors protect their turf? As the night follows the day. Should we trust the internet information scrum? That was rhetorical.

When corporations do studies, they look under the money tree rather than the tree of science. Patients are not their top priority. As you go further into this story, always ask yourself "who benefits." Industrialized healthcare is always the winner. Their entitlement has become more obvious and their crimes more flagrant during the COVID era.

CHAPTER 9
TESTOSTERONE'S FAKE NEWS

T estosterone is claimed to cause prostate cancer, heart disease, and stroke. This is all false.

~

IN 1990, CONGRESS MADE TESTOSTERONE AND OTHER ANABOLIC steroids class III controlled substances. The penalties for selling and even possessing them became felonies like those for cocaine. At the Senate hearings, representatives for the FDA, DEA, the National Institute on Drug Abuse, and even the American Medical Association all testified that these medications were safe and had important medical uses. But grandstanding about sports use prevailed. Anabolic steroids became the first Schedule III drugs without euphoric or consciousness-altering properties.

In 2016, the Food and Drug Administration tightened the regulatory pressure by slapping a "black box warning" on testosterone. It claimed that the hormone caused strokes and heart disease. From then on, they only sanctioned its use for patients with genetic, cancerous, traumatic, or chemotherapy-related damage to the testicles or brain. The FDA also alleged that it should only be used for men with blood levels below 300 ng/dl, confirmed on at least two occasions. In their eyes, other applications were illegitimate.

Two clumsily concocted articles supported this stance. But Mark Richards, MD, and Abraham Morgentaler, MD, debunked these with letters to the journals demanding their retraction. Morgentaler is the Harvard physician representing the Androgen Study Group, and Richards is a practicing hormone specialist. Both physicians also wrote letters to the FDA. Dr. Rouzier wrote a review of this issue as well. All this was ignored.

Richards' well-referenced article tells the entire story. He writes that low, not high testosterone is the major risk for heart disease. And according to a comprehensive Mayo Clinic review, testosterone *decreases* the chance of dying of heart disease.

What about prostate cancer? Dozens of studies show no relationship to testosterone, and men with higher levels have a *reduced* risk. The medical literature says testosterone supplementation is healthy. The Mayo Clinic's International Expert Consensus Resolution statement ratifies this view. A review in the Journal of the Endocrine Society (2019) describes the hormone as an anti-inflammatory.

Testosterone converts to estrogen in the body. This not only suppresses prostate cancer but has been used to treat it. In addition, prostate cancer is much more common in older men with low testosterone levels (this is circumstantial rather than definitive evidence). For more, see The Prostate Cancer Meat Grinder section of Butchered by "Healthcare" in the bonus section.

Note: after prostate removal for cancer, when the PSA drops below a level of one for a year, patients may safely take testosterone. Also, a promising report tells of testosterone used in large doses to *treat* prostate cancer by "shocking" it. This may work because testosterone is converted into high levels of estrogen, which suppress the tumor.

Some men using injectable (but not cream) testosterone have elevated red blood cell counts (RBCs). This is healthy and safe, but most physicians have the mistaken idea that it causes blood clots. In their defense, the only thing doctors commonly see that produces this finding is Polycythemia Rubra Vera (PV). This is a disease that causes strokes, heart attacks, and clotting problems, and treatment is essential if you have it. But in PV, all the blood cells—the RBCs, the platelets, and white blood cells—are elevated.

People who live at high altitudes have effects similar to testosterone users. Their bodies create extra red blood cells to allow better oxygen delivery. At sea level, a normal RBC percentage for men is 42-52%, and for women, 38-46%. In Vail, Colorado, at 8,000 feet, the average resident's count is 57%, and Sherpas living high in the Himalayas may have 68%. Neither those with testosterone-induced high RBCs nor people living at altitude have an increase in heart attacks, strokes, or blood clotting. Both groups have high testosterone, so these syndromes likely have a common cause.

Other causes of elevated RBCs without higher clotting risks include the following. In each case, all the rest of the blood cells are normal except for the number of RBCs.

✪ Chronic obstructive pulmonary disease (COPD). The extra red cells help these people get enough oxygen despite their bad lungs.

✪ Cigarette smoking. This raises red cell counts as high as 60%. These people have no other blood abnormality.

✪ There are mice that have hereditary RBC counts of up to 80%. They do not have increased blood clots.

✪ Certain heart patients have abnormal passages between

their chambers with mixing of low-oxygen blood and high-oxygen blood. This causes increased RBCs.

After 50 years of study, no medical literature has shown harm from an increase in red blood cells as long as white cells and platelets are normal.

PV may be diagnosed using the "JAK2 gene test," but it is a waste of money unless the rest of the blood cells have obvious abnormalities. The treatment is to remove blood until RBC counts are normal. Alternatively, drugs may be used to slow blood production. These have side effects.

So if your doctors discover you have a high RBC count and also know you are taking testosterone, they may claim your blood is "thick." Even if they realize you do not have PV, they may try to treat you. But this is unnecessary—the "abnormality" has no known risks.

A FEW KEY REFERENCES FOR READERS OF THE PRINT EDITION:

✪ Long-term Testosterone Therapy Improves Cardiometabolic Functioning and Reduces Risk of Cardiovascular Disease in Men with Hypogonadism: A Real-Life Observational Registry Study Setting Comparing Treated and Untreated (Control) Groups *J Cardiovascular Pharm Therapeutics* (2017)

✪ Fundamental Concepts Regarding Testosterone Deficiency and Treatment: International Expert Consensus Resolutions by Abraham Morgentaler, MD and others (Harvard), *Mayo Clinic Proceedings,* July 2016. This is a comprehensive summary of the science of testosterone for men. It should have shut down the critics, but it did not. Testosterone protects against heart disease and other health issues.

✪ YouTube summary of Dr. Morgentaler's testosterone views.

✪ The Benefits and Risks of Testosterone Therapy, a Review.

Therapeutics and Clinical Risk Management (2009). "TRT may produce a wide range of benefits for men with hypogonadism that include improvement in libido and sexual function, bone density, muscle mass, body composition, mood, erythropoiesis, cognition, quality of life and cardiovascular disease."

CHAPTER 10

GROWTH HORMONE WAS SMEARED

The human growth hormone (HGH) story is a variation of the others. The punch line is that if it was economical and unrestricted, it might be the most valuable hormone of all. It is likely the safest.

> **Steven** is a gay 72-year-old cosmetic surgeon who practices in West Los Angeles. He hangs out with a string of young, good-looking partners. Steven used testosterone, DHEA, and vitamin D for six months and improved. But he was still sore and fatigued, so he started HGH. After five weeks he said: *My sex, energy, and sleep are off the charts. I can work out again without getting sore. And I just got back from a boot camp!*

Growth hormone was used to treat a growth hormone deficient boy in the late 1950s. It made him taller, so the idea caught on. A commercial product derived from human pituitary glands became available in the late 1970s, and by 1985, 27,000 children had been treated worldwide. When a few people who received

HGH were found to be infected with fatal Creutzfeldt-Jacob disease (CJD), the use of pituitary-derived HGH was halted.

In 1985, Genentech developed an FDA-approved "recombinant" bio-identical HGH. It has never caused CJD. Since then, the industry has introduced thirteen other nearly identical products. Their prices are all exorbitant.

In 1990, Daniel Rudman published a six-month study of 21 older men taking HGH (NEJM). Compared to controls, they had an 8.8 percent increase in lean body mass and a 14.4 percent decrease in fat. This was an "anabolic" effect—a proven reversal, in a short time, of the usual aging trend toward muscle loss and fat gain.

This trial was a benchmark that spawned other research. Soon, evidence developed that the medication increased bone density, strengthened immunity, decreased cardiac risk factors, improved cardiac function, decreased cholesterol, improved mental functioning, and improved quality of life. See Appendix C for references about how growth hormone prevents Alzheimer's disease and improves cognitive function. HGH has also been used successfully to treat burns, heart failure, Crohn's disease, obesity, fibromyalgia, multiple sclerosis, ulcerative colitis, and other conditions.

Hormone physicians say these findings support using growth hormone to combat aging and improve vitality. And since most adults over 60 have about the same HGH production as people with damaged pituitary glands, they believe prescribing it is reasonable.

Unfortunately, the FDA did not agree. Human growth hormone received approved for AIDS wasting, but strangely, it is off label for most other adult applications including all the above. A 2005 JAMA commentary declared that off-label human growth hormone prescribing was illegal. And a 2019 Drug Enforcement Administration monograph claimed "anti-aging" use was illicit.

The FDA tries to dictate medical practice, which is not their job. Every physician knows that prescribing conventions allow them to treat conditions with any approved medication if they document the reason. Estimates of the total drugs used off-label range up to half of all prescriptions written. We have substantial evidence that HGH improves health, and prescribing it for aging is legitimate.

Athletes have employed growth hormone for forty years. Although it is not a controlled substance like testosterone, HGH has been heavily regulated since 1990, and the FDA does not approve it for athletic performance enhancement. Distribution or possession without a prescription is a crime. Ryan Cronin's article in the *Washington University Journal of Law and Policy* (2008) explains the thicket of confusing, politically motivated regulation restricting its use.

Costs: Modern HGH is manufactured using bacteria in vats, just like insulin. Both would be cheap if there was no patent system, but human growth hormone can cost $1000 a month. Some clinics retail it to customers, driving the price still higher. It is less expensive outside the US, but faked packaging is common, and an expert is required to distinguish counterfeits from originals. Although over-the-counter HGH pills and creams are cheap, they are frauds.

How to give and monitor growth hormone: It is injected at bedtime just under the skin into fat using a tiny 30 or 32 gauge needle five to seven days a week. Patients receive saline fluid that they insert into a bottle of HGH powder, and this preparation likely stays active for four weeks if kept refrigerated. One brand, Norditropin, comes as a pre-mixed liquid.

HGH is measured both in international units (IU) and milligrams (mg). One mg equals 3 IU. A good starting dose is .2 mg per day (.6 units). This is increased every few weeks to .4 to .6 mg a day (1.2 to 2 units). Athletes sometimes take double this dose or more. "Elite" bodybuilders often use 6 IU per day.

There is no accurate blood test for human growth hormone because the human body produces it at irregular intervals and it only lasts a few minutes in the blood. Endocrinologists diagnose HGH deficiency using an "insulin tolerance test," where they inject insulin intravenously and then measure blood sugar. This is hazardous and has caused fatalities. The "insulin-like growth factor-1 (IGF-1)" blood test is a good substitute to assess HGH. Young people have levels of about 300 to 350 ng/ml, so this has become the treatment goal for older people.

Some patients have dramatically improved their well-being a few weeks after starting growth hormone. Others feel little. Health improvements may require three to six months. Although the drug does not have the muscle-building effects of large doses of anabolic steroids, it maintains mass and keeps bodybuilders lean. They get athletic physiques without as much attention to their diet. There are rumors about champion body-builders on HGH who eat junk food all day.

Side effects: When the amount given is about the same as the body's production, HGH causes few problems except for minor swelling and occasional joint aches. Rarely, fluid buildup in the wrists causes compression of the median nerve with finger pain and numbness (carpal tunnel syndrome). This can be prevented if the dosing starts low and is increased gradually, and is reversible if the drug is stopped or the amount used is decreased.

A persistent urban legend claims that HGH causes diabetes, but a major systematic review refuted this. Despite rumors to the contrary, HGH does not cause cancer—we know because thousands of patients have been studied.

Certain pituitary tumors that make excess HGH can cause "acromegaly." These patients have bone growth with enlarged hands, feet, and faces. They can get joint pain, hypertension, diabetes, cardiomyopathy, and visual disturbances. Tony

Robbins, who is an enormous man with size 16 feet, told his audience he had one of these tumors. I was there and heard him. He said he refused to have it treated because he liked the way it made him feel and perform. No one doubts his energy level—he does his solo self-help act before live audiences for days at a time.

If huge doses of HGH are used for long periods, a few acromegaly symptoms might occur, but getting the full-blown syndrome would likely require taking high doses for years and cost millions of dollars. A minor effect is an open space that may develop between the front teeth of HGH users because the bones of their skull grew and their teeth could not. This is seen in some bodybuilders who have used human growth hormone. Arnold Schwarzenegger's photos from the mid-1960s were taken before he had this effect, so they do not show it. A gap appeared in the images from his competition period. He must have fixed his teeth about the time he was elected governor, so the most recent photographs appear normal.

Arnold was thought to be one of the first bodybuilders to combine HGH with testosterone and anabolic steroids. Later in his career, when working on a movie, he would barely sleep. His high energy level could have been partly because of the drugs.

Conclusion: Both growth hormone and insulin are manufactured using proprietary methods, which make insulin prices stratospheric and HGH nearly unobtainable. Both are bio-identical and safe, however. Properly used growth hormone might be as useful as insulin. We do not know for sure because the restrictions hamper use and research. Most of our studies are simply stories about just a few patients.

Few doctors are willing to buck their peers and the regulatory hysteria. The ones who are willing to prescribe HGH are sometimes ostracized. Once again, a natural substance with obvious, well-established functions and minimal side effects has nearly been eliminated from our formulary. Enormous forces actively oppose its use, but they are only dimly visible from my street-level view.

CHAPTER 11
FOR ATHLETES

Lance Armstrong beat the French at their national sports: drugging, lying, and cycling.* US federal prosecutors tried to fine him $100 million. Their goal was to boost their careers by destroying people, and a superstar turned villain was a perfect candidate. They spent tens of millions of taxpayer dollars and settled for $5 million—an abject loss.

Whatever you think of Armstrong, the French, prosecutors, or athletic doping, the following is clear. Over the past four decades, sports became drenched in drugs. They are integral; they are not going away, and they enhance performance. If you do not believe this, particularly if you think Armstrong is a cheater, spend 20 minutes watching mainstream strength sports such as CrossFit championships. These performers parrot Lance: "We never tested positive."

Yet the press labels Armstrong "disgraced." They never acknowledge their hypocrisy: *nearly everyone in America—including them—takes powerful prescription drugs every single day.*

*Give thought to what we do here in the US before being too critical of the French.

My mission is to improve health and longevity for people who have declining hormone levels. I recommend higher doses than most physicians, but I am not knowledgeable about sports use. If I openly advocated it, my peers would cast me out as a renegade.

An athlete's aim is to maximize performance. If you decide to supplement, begin by learning the basic information here. Then get coaching, take responsibility for your actions, and become an expert. You may be taking health risks, although the concerns are exaggerated.

As you explore what works and what is safe, be cautious and skeptical. Big Pharma, the journals, the medical mainstream, the supplement makers, and the bodybuilding industry all have conflicts of interest—they are selling something. Most have little concern about damaging you while they get rich. I would caution you, in particular, to avoid believing random articles from internet searches. Most are written by corporate sources. And most doctors who prescribe hormones have a lot of the story wrong as well.

Remember that half of the standard medical practice is questionable, and the medical journals are unreliable (see my other book, especially The Journals' Sins are the Editor's Sins chapter that is reproduced in the bonus section). Rick Collins (cgmbesq.com), an attorney who defends athletes, wrote to me about bodybuilding sources:

> [They] *(including the magazines) have been historically far, FAR closer to the truth than mainstream physicians on issues of nutrition, exercise, and ergogenic drugs. Bodybuilders saw the value of fat in the diet when doctors were still advising patients to eat "low fat" diets–poisoning them with sugar and excessive carbs. Bodybuilders knew the importance of resistance training for decades while clueless*

doctors were advocating that all you need is aerobic exercise. Bodybuilders knew steroids build muscle when medical orthodoxy insisted that steroids didn't work—and rigged studies to "prove" it. Bodybuilders knew the risks of testosterone and HGH were wildly exaggerated and distorted decades ago–while doctors STILL have no clue. Of course, the downfall of bodybuilders is the mindset of excess– "more is better."

There must be limits on the doses, but they are unclear. Testosterone produces acne, hair growth or loss, sterility, and testicular atrophy (small balls). Women may get deeper voices and enlarged clitorises. The FDA says that testosterone increases heart disease, but the studies purporting to show this are wrong. If you use estrogen and have a uterus, you must use progesterone or risk a higher chance of uterine cancer. High doses of vitamin D3 and thyroid can cause toxicity. Testosterone relatives, such as methylated or alkylated anabolic steroids, can cause liver damage. *This short list is nearly all the known problems of hormone use.*

Criminal prosecution for anabolic steroid possession is unlikely but can cost thousands of dollars and result in jail time and a criminal record. Federal and state agencies are colonized by people who waste our tax money enforcing these laws. Mail inspectors sometimes catch drugs as they are shipped into the country, and the large quantities used by bodybuilders attract attention. Gangs of federal employees spend their time posing as mail delivery people to prove steroid users ordered drugs abroad and delivered them here.

If you consider using these medications, decide what you are trying to do. Getting bigger and stronger—to a point—is a legitimate goal, even if you are not competing. But is it meaningful for you to become a better performer at the expense of violating rules? How high are the risks of being caught and disgraced? Are you a professional athlete, or is this a vanity project?

I am not implying these are ethical questions. Nor do I know how to make competitions fair when drugs are used. If we leave sports unregulated, doses will escalate to health-damaging levels. Rick Collins comments further:

> It's said that the difference between a medicine and a poison is the dose. So, while medically bringing your low testosterone levels into the normal range may be safe and greatly beneficial (let's say, with 100 to 200 mg of a prescribed testosterone ester per week), taking ten times that dose using black-market steroids, along with a cornucopia of other anabolics and ancillaries, especially for extended periods and without medical supervision or monitoring, will almost certainly NOT be good for your heart. Author's comment: serious bodybuilders start at about 1000 mg a week of injectable testosterone or similar hormones (five times the usual men's hormone replacement dose). They then "stack" or add oral steroids and other medications such as thyroid, HGH, and estrogen blockers.

The exact boundaries between harm and good are unknown. Hormone dangers are overstated or possibly nonexistent, depending on what you do. For older people, the risks of avoiding these medications are far higher than using them. The whole thing is up to you—it is your body.

This is (somewhat) exaggerated.

Many women in Los Angeles are using male doses of testosterone. I know one who injects 200 mg of cypionate every week. Another takes only oxandrolone (Anavar), a related anabolic steroid. She is setting national age-group weightlifting records. Other women are bodybuilders who achieve muscularity and definition that would be otherwise impossible. During competition season, they inject 300 to 400 mg of testosterone cypionate a week and take thyroid, diuretics, and other drugs orally.

These women love sex, feel feminine, and have lots of energy. They like their muscles and enjoy having large clitorises. Some of them asked what I thought. I told them they were in unknown territory and that there were no guarantees. I said my best guess was that they were not damaging their longevity, but that they might be permanently suppressing fertility.

Carefully consider what you are doing. Blood testing helps. Sugar, liver enzymes, cholesterol, and of course the levels of hormones themselves can be an index of what is happening to your body. Testing may be obtained without a prescription at LifeExtension.com in Florida. Your blood will be drawn at a local lab and the results emailed back to you.

Get guidance and support. Listen to your friends about your behavior, and if it changes, reconsider the doses. If you can find a knowledgeable doctor who works in sports, hold on to them and be respectful. Physicians are so conservative and regulated now that such an animal is almost a unicorn. Most doctors recommend hormone doses that are too small to help aging people, let alone make athletes perform better.

PART IV
THYROID, THE MASTER AND COMMANDER

CHAPTER 12

THYROID BASICS AND POLITICS

Thyroid "quarterbacks" the entire metabolism. It regulates and activates many body processes and is essential for energy and weight control. Borderline low or "hypothyroid" conditions are common, under-treated, and seven times more likely in women. Treatment is safe and should be general primary care rather than being stashed in a subspecialty.

> **Judy** is 40 years old: *When I was 35, I started getting depressed and was chronically exhausted. I was losing my hair and felt cold all the time. I was constipated, grumpy, and had no interest in sex. I had to direct my kids from the couch because I didn't have the energy to chase them around. All my doctors insisted my tests were normal, and that I was a hypochondriac. They finally gave me pork thyroid. After a month, my energy went from a two to a nine out of ten, and I got my husband back.*

Treatment benefits: Thyroid supplementation for appropriate patients protects against heart disease, diabetes, and memory loss. It improves hair, nails, and skin. Balancing the thyroid improves menopause symptoms, and studies have shown lower death rates for treated people.

When thyroid is low, people get fat, tired, inactive, disinterested in sex, and are more likely to develop heart disease. Erectile dysfunction is more frequent. Other symptoms include dry skin, hair loss, insomnia, brittle nails, constipation, bone and joint pain, poor concentration, trouble getting started in the morning, and cold extremities with cold intolerance.

Untreated hypothyroid patients often have medical problems including depression and coronary artery disease. Vertebral fractures are more likely, especially over 50 years old. Hypertension, premature births, rheumatoid arthritis, and metabolic syndrome have all been linked to low thyroid conditions.

Two kinds of bio-identical thyroid hormones are used for replacement, and both are vital for health. T3 has three iodine molecules and T4 has four. Desiccated pork thyroid has both types along with a few inconsequential pig thyroids. According to hormone doctors, it is the most bio-identical thyroid medication available. Physicians have used this inexpensive drug since the late 19th century.

Endocrinologists and other mainstream doctors mainly prescribe pure T4 made in the lab, which was until 2004 a patented drug. T4 converts to T3 in the body, and they believe that this creates adequate T3. But it does not work well for everyone, especially women over 40. Since T3 is far more active than T4, people who cannot convert properly have poor results when they take only T4.

For these patients, endocrinologists prefer to add synthetic T3 to the synthetic T4 instead of using the pork type, which contains both in one pill. When carefully dosed, these manufactured medications work fine, but they may not be as well absorbed as the other one. They are useful for people with a pig allergy and for Jewish or Muslim people who are not supposed to eat pigs.

T3 is stronger and shorter-acting than T4, so patients sense its effects sooner than T4. Since getting patients to return for follow-up is sometimes difficult, using a drug containing T3 may help them understand the process is worthwhile. Since thyroid's effects are long-lasting, the medication should be adjusted about once a month.

Endocrinologists train for three years in internal medicine after four years of medical school, then spend a fellowship of two or three years studying glandular functions and treatment. They take care of many conditions other than hypothyroidism. Ever since thyroid blood tests were developed, they have carefully evaluated numbers. They believe these are indispensable and possibly more valuable than the century-old art of scrutinizing thyroid patients for clues about how they are doing.

The laboratories performing these tests report their results to physicians using a bell curve determined by thousands of previous patient test values. "Normal" for most labs is thought to be somewhere in the middle. Endocrinologists believe that thyroid treatment works best when the results are near this average. However, many patients with hypothyroid symptoms feel better when their results are in the higher part of the curve. This is analogous to students graded on a college test who are happier with "As" rather than "Cs."

When people have mild symptoms but mid-normal lab tests, endocrinologists are trained to look carefully for other causes. They might recommend other drugs such as antidepressants. These have side effects, but properly dosed thyroid has none.

Few endocrinologists endorse treating people with more thyroid when their labs are in the middle of this normal range, even if they still have symptoms. But many of these patients feel far better with supplementation, and their health improves. Obesity, heart disease, cholesterol, and the metabolic syndrome decline. Female infertility, spontaneous abortion, and other complications of pregnancy decrease as well. Hundreds of references support this.

> **Paul,** initially treated with T4: *With* [the addition of] *T3, the lights went on. Within a week I could get up the stairs at home more easily. My digestive problems all vanished within days. I could think clearly and function once again. Within a few weeks, I felt like I was a different person—not the shambling wreck of a human being, old before his time. T3 on its own was the answer and the clue.*

Hormone doctors believe that mild thyroid disease with vague symptoms is everywhere. When they see the situation of mid-normal test results along with mild hypothyroid symptoms, they often recommend a "trial of therapy." This is giving the medication to see if it helps. They know that the risk-to-benefit ratio for such a trial is more favorable than trying toxic drugs such as antidepressants. They are not experimenting on their patients—a trial of therapy is a standard, accepted practice used in many medical situations. For example, this is the one-and-only strategy in psychiatry, which has no relevant lab tests.

Hormone doctors know that using T4 alone does not work well for many patients. They point out that T4 can inhibit the body's manufacture of T3 and believe that the porcine drug has a higher initial response rate. Along with evaluating physical findings and symptoms, some instruct their patients to measure morning heart rate and temperature, which is a sensitive index of improvement.

Many patients feel better when they take thyroid, even with middle-normal labs. They stop feeling cold; they feel energized, their cholesterol numbers improve, and they have more interest in sex. Since hypothyroidism is common in women over 40, this group is the most likely to have a dramatic response.

Janet is a 45-year-old physician: *I never believed that there was a difference between Synthroid and Armour until I switched. I was fat, slow, depressed, and my cholesterol was high. I got on some progesterone, and then the new thyroid made me feel great mentally. And I went from a 16 to an 8 dress size.*

Why are endocrinologists so conservative about prescribing thyroid hormone? The reason: they treat Grave's disease, a "hyperthyroid" or high thyroid condition present in two to three percent of the population. Here, antibodies stimulate the thyroid gland to release too much thyroid hormone. This causes sweating, palpitations, rapid heart rate, osteoporosis, and even atrial fibrillation, a disordered heart rhythm. This thyroid cannot simply be discontinued—reducing blood levels takes time and requires other drugs. Complications frequently develop before the situation is under control.

So endocrinologists are cautious because of their experience. They fear patients will get Grave's problems *when thyroid is used as a drug*. Here, however, the medication can easily be reduced or stopped if side effects occur. Most people quit it on their own if headaches, nervousness, jitteriness, or (more rarely) rapid heart rate occurs.

Neal Rouzier, MD, explains:

Yes, some studies showed low or suppressed TSH [which shows high thyroid hormone] *is associated with atrial fibrillation. However, that is in patients who have* Grave's Disease. *Remember that association does not prove causation. More specifically, there is no study where* administering *thyroid has "caused" atrial fibrillation.*

Other medical experiences suggest that thyroid medication is safe and predictable. For example, endocrinologists use high doses to suppress thyroid cancer without fear of complications.

And psychiatrists have treated depressed people with massive doses since the 1930s. These patients do not have thyroid disease, but they are routinely given nearly three times the usual T4 dose—.32 mg instead of .125 mg. A psychiatrist told Dr. Rouzier that he sometimes prescribes four .2 mg tablets of T4 a day, which is six times the usual dose. Since psychiatrists reserve this treatment to themselves, it does not threaten industry's profitable antidepressants.

Both these cancer patients and depressed patients have high thyroid blood levels because of the high doses but are fine. Their physicians are not concerned about osteoporosis or atrial fibrillation. And studies show no more hip fractures or decreases in bone mineral density for older women taking thyroid replacement.

Endocrinologists cite many trials that show an association between atrial fibrillation and high thyroid levels. Some studies suggest low levels cause it and others say there is no correlation. We also know that when atrial fibrillation patients are treated with thyroid, they live longer (Am J Cardiology, 2017). The sensible conclusion is that treatment should always be individualized. For sensitive people, thyroid levels should be middle-normal rather than upper-normal.

Note about names: I refer to the thyroids as T3, T4, and porcine. I avoid the following: *Synthroid* is a manufactured brand of T4 with an expired patent. It has more consistent quality than its generics. T4 is *thyroxine* or *levothyroxine*, which are the same thing. *Cytomel* is a brand of manufactured T3, and *liothyronine* is its chemical name. *Triiodothyronine* is the natural, biologically produced form of T3. These two are almost identical. Porcine brands with both T4 and T3 include *Armour, Naturethroid,* and *Westhroid.*

CHAPTER 13
MONEY DEFORMS THYROID CARE

Randy's words from a website about Armour porcine thyroid:
*I, too, was doing great on Armour. No more. They put me on
levothyroxine* [synthetic T4] *and Cytomel* [synthetic T3]. *I felt
awful, so depressed...*

Drugmakers fake and suppress their studies. Knoll
Pharmaceuticals, the Synthroid maker, hid one showing
that their drug was no better than the other thyroids. Knoll paid
more than $100 million to consumers after the ensuing class-
action lawsuit settled in 2000.

Later, the pharmaceutical companies sponsored over ten
bogus studies that purported to show porcine thyroid was no
improvement over T4. Each trial used only 1/2 grain of the pork
thyroid (30 mg), even though the proper dose is one to two
grains (60-120 mg) or more (about the same as .075 to .15 mg of
T4). Each study concluded that the tiny dose of pig thyroid did
not work. With these doses, of course, it could never work. This
type of false comparison is a routine strategy used by drugmakers to get FDA approval or to run down a competitor. For

more, see Ben Goldacre's *Bad Pharma* (2012) and my FDA chapter here.

There have been claims that the porcine thyroid manufacturing is faulty, and that this makes it inferior to Synthroid, the branded T4. However, Synthroid was recalled ten times between 1991 and 1997. This involved over 100 million tablets. The FDA requires T4 to fall within 5% of its stated potency, but most samples analyzed had far less active ingredient and some had none. Because many patients need thyroid to survive, there were hospitalizations.

In 2001, the Food and Drug Administration (FDA) issued a warning that they might pull Synthroid from the market. There were also two recalls in 2012-13 involving issues with potency, stability, and manufacturing. See Mary Shomon's website for references, including the FDA letter documenting the story. This link is offline and may have been suppressed by special interests. I had to search for it on the Wayback Machine internet archive (archive.org).

Physicians have used porcine thyroid for over a century. It was first approved by the FDA in 1939. In Thailand, it is an over-the-counter supplement. I could find only three recalls for this desiccated pig thyroid, including one started by the manufacturer in 2020 for a 13 percent drop in potency. This might have gone unnoticed, but since thyroid strength is critical, they were doing the right thing.

T4 has been available since 1927 without a formal FDA evaluation. It was given "grandfather" status in 1938 because it was assumed to be equivalent to porcine thyroid, which was considered the "gold standard." The Synthroid brand finally passed a perfunctory FDA review in 2002.

Other games: In 2000, there were efforts to get rid of Armour thyroid in the US. And in 2014, Forrest Pharma sold the Armour brand to Actavis. The new owner jacked up prices and questions developed about the drug's potency. This must have benefited AbbVie's Synthroid sales.

Each time a patient visits their thyroid doctor, they review the patient's signs, symptoms, and sometimes lab results. The dose is reconsidered and may be altered in tiny, exacting increments. Other medications, such as those for blood pressure, do not need such careful adjustment. So quality manufacturing is critically important for thyroid. Because generic T4 has a reputation for uneven quality, many specialists only use the brand names such as Synthroid. But in view of its history, it is also suspect.

Mae is 38: *Nothing was wrong, but something was not right. I don't know how many times (even having been on Synthroid [branded T4] for ten years), I'd be out with friends or family feeling as though I was freezing. My company would assure me, "It's not cold in here. Are you getting sick? Is it your thyroid disease? Shouldn't your symptoms be controlled by medication since you see your endocrinologist every three to six months?" Also, I would occasionally notice moderate amounts of hair loss in the shower. Not ridiculous, but certainly more than I would imagine a typical woman would be losing when washing her hair. I blindly trusted my endocrinologist. I didn't question her. Shame on me! I took the Synthroid, I came in for my ultrasounds every two years to monitor my nodule, and I had just been keeping quiet. After all, I'd been assured my care was "being managed." Everything in my lab work was "normal." **sigh** I didn't KNOW any better. I didn't realize I still had a chance of alleviating these symptoms. I was so used to feeling that way that they had become my new normal. Now that I've been on Naturethroid [porcine thyroid] for several months, there is no noticeable hair loss in the shower. For the first time in as long as I can remember, it was I*

*who was not cold in a room where others were the chilly ones (and I
was wearing a sleeveless dress). Incredible! :-) It's a new life. Reset
button pressed all over again. What a gloriously beautiful, crazy,
privileged, wonderful life I am blessed to lead. So grateful. But I had to
question my endocrinologist's judgment... Nothing was WRONG,
but SOMETHING clearly was NOT RIGHT... as evidenced by my
improvement in energy level, sense of overall well-being, and the
elimination of symptoms which had plagued me for years.*

I MUST NOW GUIDE YOU THROUGH THE TURF WARS—THIS IS WHERE
money changes hands. AbbVie (formerly Knoll Pharmaceutical,
bought by Abbott) controls the manufacture of T4. Drug corporations donate millions of dollars a year to endocrine organizations including the American Association of Clinical
Endocrinologists (AACE). This group creates and maintains
written standards claiming that T4 is the standard of care. It
takes an outsider to tell the truth. John Lowe, a chiropractor,
wrote:

*Why do endocrinologists resolutely endorse Synthroid as the only
brand of thyroid hormone hypothyroid patients ever need to use? The
cause is a complex interplay of factors. Prominent among them are
financial incentives to the endocrinology specialty from corporate
marketers of Synthroid. The corporations have richly funded the
specialty. He who pays the piper, of course, calls the tune. This reality
makes the proposition plausible that lavish funding by these
corporations has shaped endocrinologists' beliefs about
hypothyroidism—beliefs that are favorable, quid pro quo, to the
financial interests of the corporations, yet shown false by substantial
scientific evidence.*

These tactics work. As recently as 2013, Synthroid was the
most frequently prescribed drug in the US. Gross sales were
over $800 million that year.

The thyroid-stimulating hormone (TSH) test has been used as a weapon in this economic war. The mainstream doctors claim that it is the best single measure of thyroid therapy. Hormone doctors think it is questionable. Thousands of articles have been written debating the issue. Let me simplify it for you: the test is useless and you do not have to understand it to know hypothyroid care. The reason? TSH has no active function except as a communicator between parts of the glandular system.

Since thyroid is the "master and commander," these hormones—except TSH—have profound effects on many organs. Measuring the active ones, T3 and T4, is a precise index of what is happening to the patient. TSH numbers are frequently deceptive. Also, when thyroid hormone is taken as a medication, the TSH function is inactive.

Here is how internists and endocrine specialists use TSH. It goes higher when T3/T4 goes down and vice versa. For hypothyroid patients, they increase thyroid doses until the TSH is low but not "too low." They claim it should be between .5 and 4 (or 1 and 3 if the patient is already taking thyroid). But this may not make patients feel as good as using higher doses and getting a very low or "suppressed" TSH near zero.

These traditional doctors claim they are the only ones who appreciate the testing process. Theirs has become a geeky specialty and they must love complexity. We know that when TSH is used to direct treatment, many patients say their thyroid doses seem too low.

Trying to manage thyroid health using an indirect, slowly responsive, and inaccurate measure such a TSH is tricky. Even if the active thyroid hormones, T4 and T3, are directly measured, precisely optimizing the amount given can be challenging. Over-dosing or under-dosing may occur.

In a contradictory twist, psychiatrists and endocrinologists claim that a very low TSH is conventional for the treatment of depression or thyroid cancer, respectively. Recall that these patients never have the complications of Grave's disease. If there is a question of thyroid toxicity, the dose can simply be decreased.

TSH gives endocrinologists an excuse to be critical of the hormone physicians who pay more attention to their patients' symptoms than this lab test. This has resulted in medical board censures.

> **Mae was caught in this crossfire.** She had been on Synthroid for a decade for Hashimoto's thyroiditis. After some reading, she asked her endocrinologist about porcine thyroid. She said: *When I asked my endo about Naturethroid, you should have SEEN the expression on her face. She looked appalled that I had even brought this up. 'This is NOT the standard of care!' she exclaimed. I asked, why not? 'I am telling you. This is just NOT the standard of care. We do not even bring it up unless the patient asks, and even then, we try to discourage it. Some patients say they feel better on the natural thyroid ... yes, but most people do fine on the Synthroid. You have not complained about fatigue. Your labs are perfect. WHY ROCK THE BOAT?! If it isn't broken, do not fix it!' Long story shorter, the endo did not offer any reasonable explanation.*

Ever since the Affordable Care Act mandated electronic medical records, physicians spend a *quarter to half their time* clicking on computers just to get paid. The political pressure surrounding thyroid prescribing may force some doctors who understand the controversies to insert academic papers into their charting. This protects them but wastes yet more time.

Conclusion and further study: John Midgley, MD, a prominent thyroid scientist, summarized: "What was being done the past 35 years or so was suboptimal and has actually caused harm to patients." And a review on ThyroidScience.com concluded that TSH was an unreliable

measure of clinical thyroid function. Another reference from the BMJ (formerly the British Medical Journal) was entitled TSH is a Poor Measure of Severity of Tissue Hypothyroidism. Studies prove that symptoms of hypothyroidism with "normal" T4 and T3 levels ("subclinical hypothyroidism") are associated with an increased risk of atherosclerosis. And a set of letters published in the BMJ (2000) said that many hypothyroid patients do not feel well until their free T4 is elevated and the TSH is undetectable.

Unfortunately, patients must now not only become students of their blood tests but also of their doctors' behavior—or misbehavior. If you or one of your loved ones has a thyroid disease, learn as much as you can. Stopthethyroidmadness.com is the easiest reference. Also, see: "What Every Hypothyroid Patient Should Know about Synthroid" by Ronald Grisanti. For more detail, go to JeffreyDashMD.com. Thyroid geeks should visit thyroidpatients.ca.

Thyroid patients must find a skilled provider to help them. This field is an art, and there are complexities I have not described. If you are not careful, months—or years—can go by before your doctor sorts your problem out. Endocrinologists are true experts at treating Grave's disease, thyroid cancer, and other issues such as low cortisone. If you have thyroid symptoms, consult them, but look elsewhere if they do not make you feel great within a few months. Even if all seems well, get on the internet forums and learn all you can.

Some of the older physicians who practiced before the tests became popular are still with us. They have extensive experience evaluating hypothyroidism clinically, and their top priority is the same as yours—how you feel, look, and perform. And most of the physicians at worldlinkmedical.com are excellent choices, including the nurse practitioners.

Before trusting anyone, ask about porcine thyroid. If they hesitate, you may have learned something important. To repeat

—this is essential—never accept feeling unwell after treatment. Get a second opinion if you have any doubt.

See Appendix A, Thyroid Dosing Is An Art, for more.

Martha is 54 and had many menopause symptoms, but she only wanted to try thyroid. Why would I argue? It was a step in the right direction. I gave her a prescription for porcine thyroid, 1.5 grains a day. She did not come back to see me for a year. When Martha returned, she had lost 43 pounds (an unusual result). Her daughter told her to see me again "because he must know what he is doing." She was ready to try the other replacement hormones.

CHAPTER 14
SECRETS OF A WEIGHT CLINIC

R obert L. Morgan, NP, who practiced in the Houston area, contributed this chapter (edited by the first author). He attracted patients who failed elsewhere.

TEXAS IS THE TENTH MOST OBESE STATE, AND WE ARE PITIFULLY overweight. I have been fighting this for over 30 years, and I have been losing. Against my efforts stand big Food, doctors, big Pharma, and meddling government. This cabal wittingly or unwittingly caused the international obesity crisis. They subsidize sugary corn products, oppose fat consumption, and have cold-shouldered effective treatments including diet pills and thyroid hormone. I have had minor victories patient-by-patient, and these have cost me years of struggle.

No one is sure about the cause of the obesity pandemic. But the national directive to decrease dietary fat came out at about the time we got really overweight. This is not a coincidence—it is a cause. Other theories went as far afield as blaming bacteria

in the intestine, but for me, walking into any grocery store or convenience mart makes it obvious that the core problem is corporate food production. Who can resist the tastes, the color, the packaging, and the marketing? Everything is sweet, fat, and salty.

To put the obesity disaster into context, compare us with people in Korea and Japan. Americans who travel there are shocked—everyone looks fit! You can see their back and leg muscles through the clothes. Food habits must be more powerful than corporate influences. Even within the US, obesity rates vary from 23 percent in Colorado to 37 percent in Arkansas. These cultural differences must be a clue to causes.

The corporations are making us fat as well. Many antidepressants, diabetic medications, and synthetic hormones cause weight gain. Paid-up doctors and direct advertising force-feed us these drugs and others.

The Food and Drug Administration's function is to oversee both industries, but big Food and big Pharma control it with funding. Since the FDA is incompetent as well as compromised, it does many wrong things, and all this makes us fatter. (See *Born With a Junk Food Deficiency*, 2012, for more.)

The result is many of us have an addiction to food as powerful as others have to opioids. The morbidly obese die just like drug overdoses. I have no prayer of getting rid of marketing or food packaging. Individual patients' cooperation limits my ability to get take them off harmful medications. So I do what I can with diet pills, which suppress appetite and aid weight loss.

There is a catch. Patients gain the weight back unless their metabolism is normal or made normal using hormone supplementation. Thyroid deficiency is epidemic, and testosterone levels have been falling in our entire population. The decline of these two contributes to obesity. Replacing them for deficient people is the most effective way to keep weight off long-term, but most doctors ignore this.

Hormone replacement can kick off a gradual weight loss that continues for a decade. It works without other prescriptions, but some patients benefit from using diet pills. These are not ideal solutions, but our lives are being threatened. My program works —many of my patients have sustained a healthy weight for years.

The drug industry dictates the beliefs of traditionally trained doctors, and I have had an uphill battle against them. They vilify thyroid for weight loss and claim it is not the "standard of care." They push expensive medications and oppose simple solutions. I have suffered complaints to the medical board and have been threatened with lawsuits because I prescribe hormones. In my darker moments, I wonder if these forces oppose anything that works.

Thyroid has the potential to improve the lives of up to a third of older adults. People taking it feel more energetic, their cholesterol improves, and they sometimes lose weight. I prescribe it routinely for those who have deficiency symptoms. Some of these patients have accepted laboratory abnormalities, and others have test results I believe are abnormal, but that endocrinologists would likely ignore. I teach my patients the following basics:

✪ Taking thyroid does not guarantee weight loss, but if you need thyroid, you need thyroid! If you diet and exercise and still cannot lose weight, then you probably have a slow metabolism (low thyroid), which makes weight loss impossible.

✪ I measure both T4 and T3, and I try to optimize both. TSH is nearly a useless test, and TSH "suppression" causes no issues. With thyroid replacement, the moment the patient feels better, their TSH is always low.

✪ Most people lose weight with thyroid because they have more energy and they are getting up and moving.

✪ Many overweight patients need thyroid supplementation. If they lose weight with diet and exercise, they will gain the weight back when they stop compensating unless they take thyroid.

⊗ Surgical cures for weight loss usually fail if thyroid issues are left untreated.

ENDOCRINOLOGISTS REFUSE TO PRESCRIBE THYROID FOR MOST **obese patients.** Here are their words.

> V*ariations in thyroid function, even* [with normal] *tests…
> contribute to the development of regional obesity and the tendency to
> gain weight… thyroid hormones have been inappropriately and
> frequently used in attempts to induce weight loss in obese euthyroid*
> [normal thyroid] *subjects…* [they should not be used] *to control
> body weight except in obese hypothyroid subjects.*

They are right, but their definition of abnormal is wrong. Many people over 40 are mildly hypothyroid and would benefit from supplementation.

What about the diet pills? These got a black eye after "fen-phen" was withdrawn from the market when *fen*fluramine was implicated in heart valve problems and pulmonary hyperten-sion. This led to more than $13 billion in litigation costs. *Phen*termine, the second drug, is still available. It causes neither addiction nor withdrawal. It is FDA-approved for short-term use. This is generally interpreted as three months, but it is safe and effective for longer periods. For many more references substantiating this, see Dr. EJ Hendricks' website.

Studies of phentermine combined with topiramate, another weight loss medication, show no adverse effects on the heart. About five percent of patients have mild side effects. These include dry mouth, dizziness, taste distortion, insomnia, and constipation. This combination is patented and expensive. Topiramate is not very effective and has disadvantages, so I rarely prescribe it.

Phentermine is generic, which keeps it cheap, but the drug corporations have no motivation to legitimize it with studies. It is safe and predictable, however, and I have one of the largest experiences in the US prescribing it.

Weight loss improves blood pressure, insulin sensitivity, and cholesterol, and weight gain predicts premature death. Covid is more likely to kill you if you are fat. I am not claiming that diet pills are an ideal treatment for obesity, but something must be done. We are being slaughtered by the food and drug companies.

How can we consider taking thyroid or phentermine risky when obesity surgeons kill between 1/166 and 1/1000 of their stomach stapling patients? Where are our priorities? Are we the fattest nation in the world? How many obese people die every day from diabetes, high blood pressure, and heart disease?

Do the high-tech drugs from the medical industry work? Metformin was invented in 1922 and remains our best oral diabetes medication. It is safe, inexpensive, it modestly aids weight loss, and it may even extend lifespan. Metformin was the fourth most commonly used drug in 2018. I offer it to most of my obese patients, but half of them get diarrhea and abdominal pain and quit taking it.

The drug industry markets the "glucagon-like peptide 1 agonists" (GLP-1 drugs) for obesity treatment. I prescribed them for several years before I understood that they are marketing successes but patient failures. Most doctors, however, think they are worthwhile. You be the judge:

1) These medications aid weight loss but have significant risks.

2) Six of the seven require injection.

3) They cost over $1000 a month each.

4) The FDA says we should not use them until both metformin and another older drug have been tried.

5) Like metformin, they have significant side effects.

For example, one of these drugs, liraglutide (Victoza) costs $1126 a month. It frequently produces nausea, dizziness, low blood sugar, abdominal pain, and injection site pain. It is also associated with thyroid cancer, pancreatitis, gallbladder disease, angioedema, and kidney toxicity. Public Citizen, the Ralph Nader consumer watchdog group, wanted it banned because they said the risks were higher than the benefits.

Victoza's manufacturer, Novo Nordisk, has settled criminal cases with federal prosecutors for tens of millions of dollars. These involved allegations of bribery and other crimes (search for Novo Nordisk criminal record). They also spent $58.65 million in 2017 to pay off whistleblower lawsuits. These alleged that the company had promoted and sold Victoza for uses that were not on the product label, which is illegal for patented drugs. Settlements like these are just another day in the life of these huge corporations.

Physicians have been studying phentermine for over half a century. We know it is safe. The GLP-1 drugs have been around only for about a decade, and their toxicities are obvious. But somehow, most doctors have been brainwashed into believing that phentermine is too dangerous for common usage. So they prescribe these industry-supported, heavily advertised alternatives.

My opinions are contrary to the herd's, but my experience is massive. No pharmaceuticals are ideal for obesity except hormones for symptomatic deficiencies. Although the new diabetic medications have some positive effects, they are a net loser and should be banned.

What about diet and exercise? Food producers make marketing claims that lack of exercise is the underlying issue in obesity to draw attention away from their misdeeds and smother calls for regulation. Of course, no cure-all exists for diet. The keto idea, for example, is often unsustainable. I recommend sensible food, decreased carbohydrate consumption, and frequent exercise.

Author's note about high-fat diets: *Starting in the 1970s, Robert Adkins promoted a diet of high fat, moderate protein, and minimal carbohydrates. He directed patients to consume meats, eggs, and vegetables with no fruits or starch. There was no restriction on quantity or calories. Those who try this have a difficult few weeks until they adapt. After this, they feel a surge of energy and wellbeing. Rapid weight loss is typical. Doctors sometimes check their patients' progress with urine ketones, hence the name "keto diet."*

Does it work? Wikipedia parrots the mainstream opinion, claiming that the diet has been discredited and that long-term results are poor. But a growing subculture of keto science and successes is building. Fellow travelers include the CrossFit community. Those who continue with the strict guidelines lose weight. They have a dramatic improvement in blood insulin and other tests and can often stop diabetic and hypertension medications. Adkins recommended an eventual return to more moderate eating. But if most of these people eat so much as a strawberry, they fail the diet and go back to the way they were.

We have an unprecedented health calamity that requires novel solutions. Traditional reduced-calorie and high carbohydrate diets are nearly universal failures. Although many people do not tolerate keto diets or controlled fasting, I still think they are worth trying.

Robert L. Morgan on fasting: I weighed 220 pounds for ten years, then lost 32 pounds in eight weeks using the "one meal a day (OMAD)" plan. This means I consumed the food I ate for 24 hours during a two-hour "feeding window." The rest of the time I didn't eat. My waist measurement went from 44 to 32 inches. I have kept the weight off for over a year. Since then, I have been coaching my patients about controlled fasting and OMAD. Some benefit from simply restricting their eating to eight hours a day, or just cutting out their eating after 6 PM.

The enormous advantage of fasts is that they do not slow
metabolism. Ordinary diets decrease metabolic rate permanently, which makes obesity permanent. I instruct my patients to
listen to podcasts such as the one by Gin Stevens or
eatmostlyfat.com, which is hosted by a cardiologist. I also have
them read Jason Fung's books to learn more. His patients stop
most drugs, lower their cholesterol, and often eliminate
diabetes.

**What works best for weight loss and health improvement
—diet, exercise, or prescription medication?** Exercise is a
distant third. Of the drugs, metformin helps, but the diabetes
agents patented in the past ten years are failures. Hormone
replacement can make a huge difference—nearly every obese
person has deficiencies and can benefit. As for weight-loss diets,
the most promising ones are partial and complete fasts, but
many people cannot tolerate them. See the next chapter for other
recommendations.

Extra credit, part 1: The definition of obesity: The Body
Mass Index (BMI) is the traditional measure and has been used
for research since the 1800s. This is the weight in kilograms
divided by the height in meters. It lumps body fat and lean
muscle together and is a poor yardstick for athletes, Asians, and
Africans. It does not distinguish the harmless fat under the skin
from the more dangerous fat under the abdominal muscle wall
near the intestine. This "visceral" fat increases the chances of
diabetes and heart disease.

Since BMI can be normal even if you are very overweight,
some researchers use percentage body fat instead. This relates
more closely to heart disease, diabetes, osteoporosis, and premature death. It can be measured in several ways, from calipers to
high-tech "dual-energy X-ray absorptiometry (DEXA)" scans.
But simple measurement of waist and neck circumferences may
be as good as these other approaches.

Each method has different results, but each is useful to evaluate changes and, for the most part, internally consistent. BMI may be the best for studying populations, but we should use fat percentages to follow individuals.

Extra credit, part 2: Hormone questionnaires. These will help you communicate with your providers. If you fill them out every few months, you will see your improvement during therapy.

Do you have problems with weight gain or losing weight?	☐ Yes	☐ No
Do you occasionally feel depressed or have depressed moods?	☐ Yes	☐ No
Is your concentration decreased?	☐ Yes	☐ No
Do you have problems with occasional constipation?	☐ Yes	☐ No
Do you get cold easily or have cold hands or feet?	☐ Yes	☐ No
Have you noticed excessive hair loss?	☐ Yes	☐ No
Is your skin dry?	☐ Yes	☐ No
Do you have trouble sleeping?	☐ Yes	☐ No
Poor energy or fatigue?	☐ Yes	☐ No
Bone / Joint Pain	☐ Yes	☐ No

Before we started you on thyroid, **please circle all the symptoms** you had:

weight gain, fatigue, poor energy, depressed mood, difficulty getting started in the morning, dry skin, brittle nails, thinning hair or hair loss, poor concentration, insomnia, constipation, bone or joint pain, cold extremities or cold intolerance

Please rate your QUALITY of life **before** starting thyroid. 1 2 3 4 5 6 7 8 9 10 (1=low 10 is best)

Have your symptoms improved since we started you on thyroid? yes no

Do you feel your QUALITY of life has improved since we started you on thyroid? yes no

Please rate your QUALITY of life **taking** thyroid. 1 2 3 4 5 6 7 8 9 10 (1=low 10 is best)

Indicate any NEGATIVE side effects of the thyroid that we have not been able to correct.

- Please circle: anxious nervous jittery palpitations irritability insomnia

CHAPTER 15
A DETOUR: DIET DILEMMAS

Obesity is a true pandemic and one of the worst health disasters of our lifetime. The best treatment is unknown. Diets that are appropriate for thin people do not help the obese —advice like "eat a moderate diet" and "don't eat between meals" is useless for them. Intermittent fasting and the Adkin's-type diets work but require weeks to months of adjustment and need to be continued indefinitely.

AGRICULTURE IS A GREAT GIFT THAT IS SAVING THE WORLD. FARM productivity has exploded in the last 50 years. Worldwide famine deaths have crashed. The chart below is from Steven Pinker's phenomenal *Enlightenment Now* (2018):

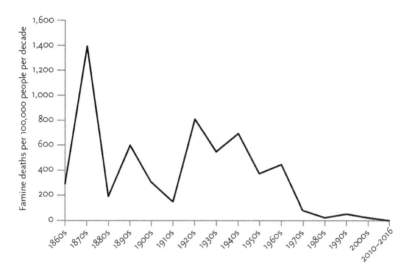

Figure 7-4: Famine deaths, 1860–2016

Sources: *Our World in Data,* Hasell & Roser 2017, based on data from Devereux 2000; Ó Gráda 2009; White 2011, and EM-DAT, *The International Disaster Database,* http://www.emdat.be/; and other sources. "Famine" is defined as in Ó Gráda 2009.

Hybrid crops and mechanization have driven up corn yields. There were 20 bushels per acre in 1980, but by 2019 this increased to 160. Other crops show similar trends.

Other advances have paralleled and were likely the result of abundant food. Global literacy was 55 percent in 1950 and rose by 5 percent a decade after that. It is now 86 percent. No rational person—outside of an oddball billionaire or two—still worries about the "population bomb." The number of people in the world is projected to be 9.7 billion by 2064, but this will decline to 8.8 billion by 2100.

These trends debunk the media disaster-mongering. But against this optimistic tide, we have obesity. The daily calories food producers supplied to US citizens rose from 2900 per person in 1961 to 3700 today. Adult caloric requirements range from 2000 for sedentary women to about 3000 for a few active men. Big Food must either export the excess or force-fed it to us using marketing. In 1980, 15 percent of us were obese, but this number is now a third. Overweight people are another third (CDC).

Authorities have recommended low-fat diets for forty years. "Saturated" animal fats increase blood levels of "bad" cholesterol (LDL), which was assumed to be evidence that a high-fat diet caused heart disease. So in 1985, the Surgeon General's Report on Nutrition and Health recommended dietary fat restriction. When the Food Pyramid came out in 1992, these guidelines went mainstream. Later versions were promoted in 2005 and 2011. It all sounded sensible—the government was trying to help. What could go wrong?

Food Guide Pyramid

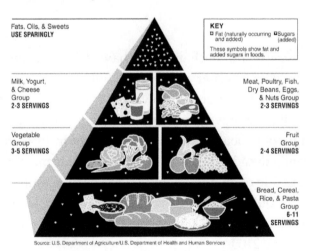

Ideas from 1992

Confusing changes in 2005

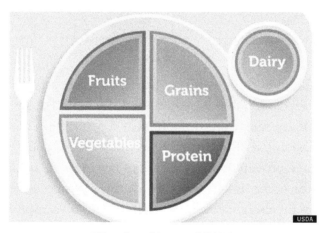

What does this mean? (2011)

OUR OBESITY BEGAN ABOUT THE SAME TIME AS THE FOOD PYRAMIDS promoted low-fat and low animal fat diets. The for-profit food companies helped market these ideas, peddling cheap manufactured fats and processed sugar under "low fat and cholesterol" labels. The graph below shows that how this correlated with the development of our obesity.

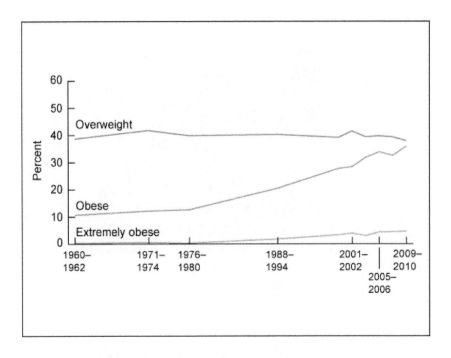

Although the consensus is not complete, powerful evidence has now developed that we eat too little fat, and that saturated animal fats are safe. Even though meat consumption raises bad LDL cholesterol, it also raises the "good" one, HDL. Dozens of studies have proven that this diet does not cause heart disease. Others showed no association with death or stroke, either. Eating less fat also encourages carbohydrate consumption, which increases heart attack risks.

Cholesterol numbers are related to atherosclerosis, but changing them with drugs or diet is less beneficial than was originally thought. Statin medications, for example, lower the bad LDL cholesterol but do not decrease heart attack deaths enough to justify their side effects. They are only useful in a few narrow circumstances. (*Butchered by "Healthcare,"* 2020.)

Food manufacturers use high pressure and temperature to synthesize the hazardous "partially hydrogenated" oils and "trans fats" that have infested our foods for a century. The process transforms cheap vegetable oils into tasty solids with seductive textures and "mouth feel." These are ideal for cooking because they tolerate high temperatures. When baked into cookies and sweets, they can sit for years in colorful packages on store shelves without getting rancid. They are commonly found in:

1) Margarine
2) Vegetable shortening (often used in restaurant deep fryers)
3) Many packaged snacks
4) Many commercial baked foods
5) Ready-to-use dough
6) Many fried foods
7) Coffee creamers, dairy and nondairy

The good news now is that these synthetically altered oils have been partially banned in many countries and some states. The US requires labels and is supposedly phasing them out.

The US Department of Agriculture (USDA) and the Food and Drug Agency (FDA) are our food regulators. They promoted the now obsolete idea that animal fat caused heart disease and recommended replacing butter with cheap, processed vegetable oil. These regulators are captives of big Food's money and work closely with their puppet masters. For more, see *Born With a Junk Food Deficiency* (2012) by Martha Rosenberg.

The same author wrote, "Big corporations like Nestle are aggressively making people even fatter across the globe" in *Salon* (2017). She tells how food companies market soft drinks and other junk foods with complete disregard for health consequences. Duff Wilson's article (Reuters, 2012) elaborated. Coke and other corporations hijacked the World Health Organization's policies using donations.

Yearly US sugar intake increased from 120 pounds in 1970 to over 150 pounds currently (note the correlation with obesity on the graph above). This is $2/5^{th}$ of a pound per day—700 calories, and a third of it came from soft drinks. This total is the highest in the world and a quarter higher than the next biggest users, Germany, Netherlands, Ireland, and Australia.

Dietary sugar is over a fourth of the calories we consume, and this doubles our risk of dying from heart disease. Sugar consumption causes diabetes, fatty liver, increased triglycerides —and obesity. People with type 2 diabetes, which is also caused by obesity, have twice the Alzheimer's rates as those with normal glucose levels. Our sugar consumption is likely a bigger health hazard than even processed oils.

Corn is used to create most of the sugary additives in our packaged food. The US spends $5 billion a year subsidizing the crop's production with federal farm supports. These began ninety years ago as a well-meaning attempt to protect farmers from bankruptcy by dampening fluctuations of crop yields and markets. In recent decades, the system mutated into a mandate to overproduce sugar. The land in the US now devoted to corn cultivation is an area 80 percent as large as California. A few monster agricultural producers pay lobbyists tens of millions of dollars a year to keep it all going.

Industry gave us a third damaging "food" class—artificial sugars. The first artificial sweetener, saccharin, was invented in the late 1800s and was in common use for most of the twentieth century. The FDA banned it in 1977 because it caused cancer in lab rats. Indigestible sugars like this, just like real sugar, stimulate the body to produce insulin, which drops blood sugar and makes people hungry. This promotes a vicious cycle of more junk food consumption and more obesity.

~

WHAT DIET WORKS?
The vegans are vocal, but their evidence is slender. Michael Greger, an influential herbivore, makes convincing, rational

arguments favoring vegetable diets and against fat consumption at NutritionFacts.org. These diets make some people feel great, and Greger has a huge following. His latest book, *How Not to Diet*, includes over 5000 citations. Some are valid, but others back oddball ideas. For example, Greger reports that consuming chili peppers burns a few extra calories a day.

Greger is an "ethical vegan." This means he believes animal lives matter and that we are murdering them. A plant-eating friend patiently clarified their doctrine for me. She said that meat-eating increases carbon usage and "all the scientists agree" that this will cause planetary apocalypse. If this is true, it renders all other considerations frivolous. My friend adds that she does not care if these eating habits damage her health.

Although I am not an expert on climate change, my study of healthcare corruption taught me that conclusions based on small numbers are suspect. Likewise, divining the future is a game that most experts lose. I also have suspicions that other scientists are as subject to muddy thinking and financial influences as the people in medicine. And after all the falsehoods the media has fed us recently, I have trouble believing anything they claim as fact. So I leave these considerations to the reader. For myself, I chose not to imagine that I am inside a dystopian science fiction novel.

The "China Study" (the China-Oxford-Cornell Study on Dietary, Lifestyle and Disease Mortality Characteristics in 65 Rural Chinese Counties) was a massive epidemiological investigation of nutrition conducted in the 1980s. It concluded that dining on animals was harmful to the heart and caused cancer. The Study advocated consuming carbohydrates and, like the other sources of its day, was critical of cholesterol. Vegetable advocates oft quote it.

But the science supporting the superiority of vegan or vegetarian diets is questionable, and many studies undermine it. A meta-analysis with 37,000 participants showed higher rates of bone fractures and osteoporosis (1) in vegans and vegetarians. They had lower bone density (2). Another study of 42 European countries showed that the populations that ate more fat and meats had lower heart disease and death rates than those with higher carbohydrate consumption (3). An interview study of 1300 Australians found "a vegetarian diet is associated with poorer health (higher incidences of cancer, allergies, and mental health disorders), a higher need for health care, and poorer quality of life" (4). Vegans have a higher overall death rate in both Australia (5) and Britain (6). Harriet Hall's article in *Science Based Medicine* (2013), Death as a Foodborne Illness Curable by Veganism, is a skeptical, comprehensive review.

For readers of the print edition: references for this paragraph are at the end of the chapter.

We now eat anything, any time we want. We often consume food from the time we arise until we go to sleep at night—16 hours a day or more. Contrary to the "eat many small meals" myth, this is unhealthy.

Human studies support various types of fasting (*Weightlifting is a Waste of Time*, 2020, has many references). During the period that people do not eat, their bodies heal. They produce higher levels of testosterone and growth hormone. These have "anabolic" effects that stimulate muscle growth and fat loss.

Mice experiments studying food deprivation have been performed as far back as 1945. One recent study showed extended lifespans and improved health when the animals were fed over eight hours rather than the entire day. And the mice lost weight even though the number of calories they consumed was the same.

Humans with a modicum of restraint can simply eat for 8 hours in a row and then quit. For example, they might consume food only from 11 AM to 7 PM. This has been successful for many if they avoid junk food. Some do well if they simply cut out eating after six PM. The next step in this sort of restricted diet is to limit food to only two to four hours a day. This is popularly called "one meal a day" (OMAD). Some people require longer fasting periods of up to several days to produce significant weight loss.

These are complex issues and there is no consensus. John Ioannidis, the renowned Stanford study design expert, says the trials about the effects of diet on health are flawed. He believes these are too small, not randomized, or otherwise biased. Observational surveys such as the China Study show correlation and not causation. This means that the Chinese likely have less heart disease because of factors other than diet.

To illustrate how little we know, recall the last chapter's discussion of Adkin's-type diets. These consist solely of meat, eggs, cheese, and fat. According to mainstream medicine, Atkins was discredited (he died, after all). But patients who can tolerate this method long-term have declining cholesterols and can quit most or all of their diabetes and high blood pressure medications. Some eat hamburger patties from fast-food restaurants— and it works.

Conclusions:

✪ Animal fat consumption has no special damaging effects on the heart. Vegan diets have not been proven to be the healthiest, but they work well for many. Results vary and there are no rules about what is best for everyone.

✪ Eating all day promotes weight gain and is less healthy than only having one or a few meals.

✪ Americans are using huge quantities of sugar, and this a cause, possibly the primary reason, for our heart disease. It is hard to avoid—for example, there is a lot of sugar in dried cranberries and beef jerky. Exactly how much you can safely consume is unknown.

✪ Partially hydrogenated (trans) fats also cause heart disease. Try to avoid it completely. This stuff is leaving the marketplace, but watch out for it anyway. If "hydrogenated oil" is listed, it could contain the partially hydrogenated type.

✪ Monounsaturated fats such as olive, almond, coconut, and avocado oils are traditionally thought to be the healthiest choices for cooking. But they are no better than animal fats such as butter.

✪ Avoiding most restaurants is safest. They want our business more than they care about our health. Many serve the least expensive and most palatable fats along with all the sugar possible. They put salt in everything, which has effects on high blood pressure and stomach cancer.

✪ In grocery stores, you must ignore tens of thousands of alluring, colorful packages. Check the labels but always remain skeptical. Processed foods are unhealthy and hard to evaluate. Frozen, packaged, and canned foods usually contain undesirable ingredients.

✪ Buy the foods you understand and recognize. Meat, fruit, nuts, dairy, whole grains, and vegetables are the best choices.

A few references for the "Vegans are vocal" section:

1) Veganism, vegetarianism, bone mineral density, and fracture risk: a systematic review and meta-analysis. Isabel Iguacel et al. *Nutrition Reviews*, Volume 77, Issue 1, January 2019, Pages 1–18.

2) Veganism and osteoporosis: A review of the current literature. Annabelle M Smith MS RN OCN. *International Journal of Nursing Practice* Volume 12, Issue 5 p. 302-306.

3) Food consumption and the actual statistics of cardiovascular diseases: an epidemiological comparison of 42 European countries, Pavel Grasgruber, Martin Sebera, Eduard Hrazdira, Sylva Hrebickova & Jan Cacek (2016) *Food & Nutrition Research*, 60:1, DOI: 10.3402/fnr.v60.31694

4) Nutrition and Health – The Association between Eating Behavior and Various Health Parameters: A Matched Sample Study. Nathalie T. Burkert et al. *Plos One*. February 7, 2014 https://doi.org/10.1371/journal.pone.0088278

5) Vegetarian diet and all-cause mortality: Evidence from a large population-based Australian cohort - the 45 and Up Study. Seema Mihrshahi et al. *Prev Med.* . 2017 Apr;97:1-7. doi: 10.1016/j.ypmed.2016.12.044. Epub 2016 Dec 29.

6) Mortality in British vegetarians: results from the European Prospective Investigation into Cancer and Nutrition (EPIC-Oxford). Timothy J Key et al. *The American Journal of Clinical Nutrition*, Volume 89, Issue 5, May 2009, Pages 1613S–1619S, https://doi.org/10.3945/ajcn.2009.26736L

PART V
THE BAD, THE GOOD, AND THE TROUBLESOME

CHAPTER 16
HORMONE BLOCKERS RUIN HEALTH

Proprietary hormone "blocker" drugs are immensely profitable. These medications are used to treat cancer but produce hormone deficiencies that damage health. This is a questionable tradeoff that should be considered only by experienced providers with the full understanding and consent of their patients. It should be an "art of medicine" area rather than an accepted standard of care for certain cancers.

Some bio-identical hormones have been used as cancer therapies. If we stopped using the blockers and instead used these hormones, we might help more patients.

Two types of estrogen blockade are FDA-approved for "estrogen sensitive" breast cancer. "Aromatase inhibitors" (AIs) such as anastrozole (Arimidex) block or suppress the conversion of testosterone to estrogen, which can stimulate the growth of breast tissue. Selective estrogen receptor modulators (SERMs) such as tamoxifen stick to the body's estrogen receptors in the tissues. This prevents estrogen from activating breast cancer cells and making them grow.

The AI and SERM drugs are both used to treat breast cancer in women with estrogen receptor-positive tumors. Oncologists sometimes give AIs to women who have not yet developed cancer but who are at high genetic risk for it. SERMs are also used to prevent new and recurrent tumors in breast cancer patients. They are sometimes given for years.

SERMs are a health disaster. These drugs trade one risk, cancer, against another—dying of Alzheimer's, cardiovascular disease, or other aftermaths of hormone deficiency. The blockers also increase the risks of strokes, bone loss, diabetes, and endometrial cancer. With low hormone levels, many patients have trouble thinking, and most feel terrible. Other common symptoms include fatigue, hot flashes, night sweats, and mood swings. Both AIs and SERMs cause these. There are other disadvantages—SERMs often quit working after a few years, and the AIs cause chronic joint pain.

Cancer studies are primarily designed to look at what happens to the malignancy, and sometimes the patients get nearly ignored. Treatments are useless if you die sooner of something else, even if the cancer is shrinking or cured as you pass away.

Testosterone blockers are used to treat prostate cancer, but they may cause more illness and death than they prevent. These "LHRH agonists," such as Lupron and other "chemical castration" agents, decrease testosterone and estrogen by interfering with the brain (pituitary) hormone that stimulates their manufacture. The resulting low hormone levels cause hot flashes, irritability, insomnia, and headaches along with major health deterioration. Otis Brawley, head of the American Cancer Society until 2018, wrote:

...widespread use of [the anti-] hormonal agents is causing men to die of cardiovascular disease and diabetes before they would ordinarily die of prostate cancer... If urologists stop prescribing these drugs as widely as they used to, we will see deaths from prostate cancer start to inch up. That could be good news. Some of the men who would have been killed earlier by strokes and heart attacks caused by hormonal treatments of their asymptomatic disease would now be living long enough to die of their prostate cancer.

— OTIS BRAWLEY, *HOW WE DO HARM (2012)*

Hormone blockers are marketed as treatments for balding. Propecia (finasteride) is the best-known of these FDA-approved drugs. It blocks the conversion of testosterone to dihydrotestosterone (DHT), a vital but less well-known hormone related to testosterone and associated with hair loss. The dose is one milligram a day. Some patients economize by using a pill cutter to divide the five mg tablets that are approved for prostate enlargement.

Eucapil is another DHT blocker that is applied to the scalp. The manufacturer claims it is not absorbed into the rest of the body. It is not available in the US but may be available on websites. Avodart (dutasteride) .5 mg is another similar medication. It is long-acting, so patients take it twice a week. These medicines thicken the hair on the crown of the head. They take many months to work and do not help if you are already bald.

Notes: 1) Blood donation can cause congenital disabilities if pregnant women have a transfusion from someone who is taking these drugs. 2) Finasteride may decrease the PSA blood test results by half.

Finasteride has major side effects, including depression, impotence, and shrinkage of the penis and testicles. Merck, the manufacturer, alleges these are temporary, but confidential court documents proved they covered up these disasters to protect sales. Those who are already taking testosterone have less likelihood of these effects. If you must use these drugs, take only the ones applied to the scalp and hope they have no effects on the rest of your body.

Most bodybuilders and many others still think estrogen is a woman's hormone. They believe it is not proper for men and that it should be blocked. Many physicians believe this as well. It sounds logical, but they are wrong—meathead reasoning like this is not science. And a few bodybuilding sources are beginning to understand the perils of blockers.

These ideas may have been started by bodybuilders who inject huge testosterone doses and get the side effects when it converts to estrogen. High estradiol levels cause gynecomastia, which is breast overgrowth (cream testosterone seldom causes this). Anastrozole .5 mg taken twice a week may control it, but it should be stopped as soon as the nipples are no longer sore. Tamoxifen is another alternative. But after a few months, the health risks of these drugs outweigh any utility. Surgical removal of the tissue is the best treatment.

Katya Rubinow wrote about estrogen in *Sex and Gender Factors Affecting Metabolic Homeostasis, Diabetes, and Obesity* (2017). She concluded this hormone helps maintain men's good health and lean body weight. Those with low levels have less interest in sex and may get fat. They have increased chances of stroke, heart disease, depression, diabetes, memory loss, high cholesterol, and osteoporosis. Rubinow also reviewed the damage caused by estrogen blockers.

When men use estrogen as a medicine, every study showed improved health and decreased risks of heart disease. Favorable effects are seen on bone, brain, heart, lipids, inflammation, Alzheimer's disease, and visceral fat (the excess surrounding abdominal organs).

Young, healthy men have high levels, and these are associated with excellent health, low heart disease rates, and good bone quality. So a few hormone doctors now supplement estrogen in adult men if giving testosterone does not raise estrogen levels enough. The jury is still out on this practice.

Note about a confusing controversy: Overweight men have high estrogen blood levels and also elevated risks for coronary artery disease (CAD). Some sources misinterpret this as evidence that high estrogen *causes* CAD. This is wrong—visceral fat manufactures estrogen and causes unhealthy metabolic derangements such as diabetes. Estrogen is an innocent bystander and not the reason for the health problems.

The medical community has over 50 years of experience giving men testosterone shots, which raise estrogen levels. No acceptable study shows harm. Hundreds show that testosterone benefits both men and women. Men have intellectual improvement with testosterone—but not when estrogen blockers or AIs are added. Low estrogen and testosterone levels predict earlier death for men.

When supplementation increases a woman's estrogen level to about 70 pg/ml, her cholesterol typically declines. And when testosterone raises older men's estrogen to around 50-70 pg/ml, their cholesterol numbers improve as well. These levels are usual in healthy younger men. Lower cholesterol suggests lower heart disease risks.

Although many sources support estrogen blockers, do not believe everything you read. Wikipedia, for example, has an article celebrating their virtues and belittling estrogen's importance for men. Its only reference is an advertising newspaper, *Life Extension Magazine*. A pharmaceutical shill or a physician hypnotized by the industry narrative likely wrote it:

> *Excess estradiol in men can cause benign prostatic hyperplasia, gynecomastia, and symptoms of hypogonadism. It can also contribute to increased risk of stroke, heart attack, chronic inflammation, prostate enlargement, and prostate cancer.*

Despite the science condemning these drugs, the blockers are deeply rooted in medical mythology. Given their profitability, driving a stake through their hearts is nearly impossible.

Still not convinced? Here is Dr. Rouzier from his Power-Point presentation:

Estrogen protects against:

- Bone loss & osteoporosis
- Alzheimer's Disease & dementia
- CVD, DM, IR
- No study supports lowering estrogen in men
- No study supports that high levels are harmful
- All studies support benefit to estrogen optimization; don't lower estrogen!
- Fifty years of studies demonstrate that raising testosterone levels, with the subsequent and simultaneous increase in estrogen levels from aromatization, is not harmful

- Normal estradiol level in men 10-55 (menopausal women 10-30 pg/ml)
- Typical levels on testosterone therapy run 50-70 = therapeutic levels in both men & women
- Treat elevated estradiol levels only if symptomatic (ie: gynecomastia)
- Low levels are harmful in both men and women.
- Estradiol level of young men averages 75.

Testosterone/Estrogen Imbalance

- Estrogen levels increase with testosterone administration.
- No study has ever demonstrated any harm in raising estrogen.
- All studies show benefit to raising both estrogen and testosterone.
- All studies demonstrate harm of low estradiol in men: increased risk of CAD, CVA, osteoporosis, depression, DM- all which occur with LHRH agonists

- Optimal estrogen levels are associated with less CAD, morbidity & mortality.
- Therefore do not fear estrogen in spite of media hype claiming a benefit to lowering estrogen- this is definitely harmful
- All literature to date demonstrates no harm of elevated estrogen when testosterone is administered
- All literature to date demonstrates harm when estrogen is lowered

CHAPTER 17
HORMONE THERAPY "MAGIC"

T he following stories seem too good to be true, but you can verify them using the citations and internet searches.

DO HORMONES IMPROVE SEX? YES. TESTOSTERONE HAS OBVIOUS effects for nearly everyone, and progesterone helps women. Estrogen improves sexuality for both men and women. Some hormone doctors give older men one or two mg a day to raise their levels to the normal youthful numbers of about 70-90 pg/ml. This does not feminize them. When thyroid is dosed to produce blood levels at the top of the "normal" lab range, many men and women report more interest. (I have experienced this.) And HGH produces sexual improvement for many users.

Oxytocin is another hormone that is well-known as a female lactation or breast milk stimulant. It is found in both men and women and has effects on sexual arousal, bonding with children, and romantic attachment to partners. Researchers think it reduces fear, facilitates trust, and might treat depression.

Oxytocin is sometimes used to treat delayed ejaculation in men. My friend Steven, 78, told me he had trouble until he tried it. (It did not work for me.) He said, "Bob, I feel like a teenager now. I need to do math in my head to avoid finishing too early. It's great!"

For women, oxytocin works something like Viagra for men. It is available in an expensive, proprietary nasal spray. The drug is bio-identical, so it cannot be patented, and compounders make an economical 20 mg pill.

To complete this story, Viagra and Cialis (which are not hormones) improve male erections and are relatively nontoxic. Viagra lasts about 8 hours, while Cialis may last up to 36 hours. Potential issues include flushing, headaches, stomach upset, flu-like symptoms, and several other less likely issues. Viagra comes in 50 and 100 mg pills, but compounders sometimes use 10 mg combined with 10 to 20 mg of Cialis. When used together, the two drugs may have a bigger effect than either taken alone, and the low doses cause few side effects.

Compounders invented another stimulant for women that they market as "scream cream." One preparation contains Viagra 3% and nitroglycerin 0.2% in an ointment. This is applied to the clitoris 30 minutes before sex. Others add aminophylline, an asthma drug that dilates blood vessels. I have heard from reliable sources that these concoctions work.

Can natural hormones be used to treat hair loss? What works best for hair loss is unclear, but hormone blockers are not the only way to treat it. Balancing and optimizing testosterone may be the best method to thicken women's hair and prevent thinning. Deficiency can cause hair loss, but using high doses might as well. Some believe that taking testosterone causes balding in both men and women. Also note: For men, supplementing with cream testosterone may cause more hair loss than injections because it raises DHT more. Switching to injectable may grow hair back.

Low thyroid conditions are well known to cause hair loss. Optimizing the thyroid helps hair quality and thickness for both men and women.

Hair transplantation is a minor surgical procedure that works. Hair roots are removed from the "permanent" hair areas in the back of the head and placed into the front. By now (2021), I would be bald on top without my 2500 grafts. Men with a well-defined hair loss pattern have the best results. Most women have diffuse thinning, so their outcomes are not as good, so hormone solutions should be considered first. For those on a budget, Turkey has many economical hair transplantation clinics with great reputations.

For *excess* hair: Women may be successfully treated with metformin, spironolactone, birth control pills, and/or oral estrogen. Spironolactone somehow produces more healthy hair growth for them. It can both improve scalp hair thickness and decrease excess hair. It is a mild diuretic, anti-inflammatory, and testosterone blocker.

Can hormones be used to treat cancer? Yes. Testosterone suppresses breast cancer. Oral estradiol is safe and efficacious for treating prostate cancer. Patients using these hormones do not get damaging deficiency syndromes. Whether they work better than industry's conventional therapies is unknown. Costly studies will never be done because human hormones can rarely be patented—they are unprofitable compared to patent drugs.

Estrogen blockers are conventional therapies for estrogen-sensitive breast tumors. But these cause menopause symptoms and, over time, ruin health. Since testosterone is broken down into estrogen, traditional doctors think that using it for these cases is improper, especially if the patients are taking blockers.

Rebecca Glaser, MD, published her successful experience treating breast cancer using implantable pellets combining testosterone and a blocker drug. She placed these under the skin close to the cancers. Charles Mok, DO, shrank a woman's breast cancer 75 percent in six months using testosterone pellets (personal communication. He wrote *Testosterone, Strong Enough for a Man, Made for a Woman, 2018*). Testosterone shrinks breast cancer in animals as well.

I have heard from Dr. Glaser's patients that she treats breast cancer patients with about three times the customary menopause testosterone pellet dosage—about three mg per pound. This likely produces blood levels over 600 ng/dl. For reference, postmenopausal women receive a pellet dose of one mg per pound, which produces blood levels of 200 to 300 ng/dl. This makes most women feel great (recall my superwomen). The usual pellet dose for a man is 10 mg per pound. This may produce blood levels of 1500 ng/dl. Weekly injections of inexpensive testosterone cypionate provide similar effects as pellets.

Side effects: Recall that high doses of testosterone for women potentially cause deep voices, enlarged clitorises, and active, possibly overactive sexuality. The women I know who use these doses for athletics do not mind, but they dislike hair growth and acne. These may be treated with laser hair removal and acne medications including spironolactone.

Synthetic progestins such as Provera cause some breast cancer, but bio-identical progesterone is at worst neutral. No published literature recommends against using it for breast cancer patients. One idea favoring it is that young women with high blood levels do not get cancer.

You can find physicians online who treat breast cancer with testosterone. Consult them over the phone if they are distant. Study Glaser's hormonebalance.org for more—she is a leader.

Should hormone therapy be used for breast cancer survivors? Yes—over 50 published studies confirm this. The mainstream recommendation is to wait five years after diagnosis before starting treatment, but some sources say to only wait one year if there is no tumor extension beyond the capsule of the armpit lymph nodes. Some studies have shown double the breast cancer recurrence rate in women who are left untreated.

I'm taking Prozac, Xanax, and Zyprexa for depression. Should I consider hormones instead? Yes. Estrogen, progesterone, testosterone, DHEA, vitamin D, and human growth hormone have antidepressant effects. Recall that thyroid (T3) has been used to treat depression since the 1930s and works the best.

The drug companies and the mental health industry now claim that a double-digit percentage of Americans is depressed. But the drugs they recommend are addictive and toxic. In your case, Zyprexa is an "atypical antipsychotic" medication that was originally developed for insanity but is now commonly used for depression. Like the other drugs in its class, it *decreases the average lifespan by ten to twenty years.*

Prozac is an addictive antidepressant that occasionally causes violence and suicide. This was known by the manufacturer at the time of its approval. Xanax is an anti-anxiety medication that is at least as addictive as the others. According to its original FDA approval studies, it does more harm than good after only a few weeks of use. This finding was ignored when the drug was approved.

Grab-bags of medications like these are given to almost anyone who goes to see a psychiatrist. Withdrawal from each of these drugs is often agonizing and may require tapering doses over many months. The symptoms of the original problem, such as depression and anxiety, return during the withdrawal process.

For support of these statements, see the Living on Planet Psych chapters of *Butchered by "Healthcare."*

My doctor says I have polycystic ovarian syndrome (PCOS), and I can't get pregnant. What can I do? This affects ten percent of premenopausal, reproductive-age women. No-one is sure what causes it. People with PCOS often have:

✪ Irregular or prolonged menstrual periods

✪ Acne, baldness, extra hair, and high testosterone levels

✪ Ovaries with cysts that do not make eggs

✪ Obesity or at least weight gain (weight loss helps)

✪ Heart disease, cancer, and the metabolic syndrome

Treatment is effective and makes most women feel great. We supplement T3, DHEA, and progesterone until the blood levels are high-normal. Progesterone levels should be raised to at least 10 to 20 ng/dl, which may require 200 to 600 mg a day or more. We usually divide the dose and give it twice a day for these patients. Appropriate candidates achieve fertility nearly every time. This is harmless, but few in the medical mainstream know about it.

Are my hormones making me gain weight? Thyroid, estrogen, HGH, testosterone, and DHEA promote weight *loss* and improve cholesterol. Their use reduces the bad visceral fat surrounding abdominal organs. A potbelly is terrible for your health because the fat in this location activates diabetes and coronary artery disease.

Over longer periods, testosterone works better than any diet drug. When 656 men from Boston and Germany took testosterone, they lost weight gradually for a full decade. Some physicians advertise these effects. Search for "testosterone and weight loss" to see dramatic images.

Women gain about ten pounds after menopause if they do not take hormones and five pounds if they do. Some are fluid retention, and diuretics treat this effectively.

I take estrogen but still have pain during sex. What can I do? Oral estradiol may not entirely protect the vagina, but a compounded troche inserted into the vagina will help. The best ones combine estradiol one mg with DHEA 20 mg in the dissolvable suppository. This improves sexual interest along with treating menopausal symptoms. Weaker doses, such as estradiol

.1 mg combined with DHEA 10 mg, usually cure pain with sex, but the effects are limited to the vagina.

The little waxy tablet dissolves immediately. One woman told me, "I didn't want to use that thing, but it turned out to be easy, and it made me feel sooo good." Estring and the Femring are the patented delivery systems. Recall, they are plastic estrogen slow-release devices that are left in the vagina for months.

Can I use hormones to treat my fibromyalgia and chronic fatigue syndrome (CFS)? People with this may be miserable and unproductive for years. Symptoms can include headache, sore throat, joint pain, and tender muscle points. Some have poor memory, prominent lymph nodes, and an inability to concentrate. Many feel terrible after exercise and remain fatigued after sleeping. Some sources claim these syndromes affect two percent of US citizens.

CFS baffles physicians. Some believe these patients are psychiatric cases. Doctors usually give them given trials of anti-depressants. Occasionally, doctors find Lyme disease, polymyalgia rheumatica, heavy metal toxicity, or another treatable condition. Some patients believe they suffered permanent damage from using the Ciprofloxacin (fluoroquinolone) type of antibiotic. These are toxic and overused, so this is possible.

Prescribing thyroid, estrogen, progesterone, DHEA, and testosterone may improve CFS symptoms. Raising blood levels from the low-normal to the high-normal range may be necessary.

> **Myrna** is a chronic fatigue patient who says she improves 75 percent when she takes hormones. Her current medications include Armour thyroid, 120 mg in the AM, progesterone 225 mg twice a day, and testosterone pellets, 150-200 mg every four months.

This is Myrna's video story.

For patients who have not responded to other hormones, sometimes a low dose of cortisone improves CFS symptoms. For those who can afford it, HGH might also help. Jacob Teitelbaum's book *From Fatigued to Fantastic* (1998) is still relevant and offers hope.

> Dr. Rouzier adds: *Sometimes free T3 levels of 5.5 or higher are needed for symptomatic relief of CFS* [4.2 is the upper range of normal]. *I monitor the physical exam for hyperthyroidism and encourage twice daily thyroid use. I use porcine thyroid* [which has both T3 and T4] *first, then add Cytomel* [T3] *as needed. I also use cortisone up to 10 mg twice a day. Although this does not shut off the body's natural production, 20 mg twice a day would. Once symptoms improve, I gradually discontinue this over three months. If the patient has low blood pressure, another hormone, Florinef .1 mg twice a day, may help.*

I have osteoporosis. Can hormones help me? This is a major health issue for elders. Twenty percent of those over 65 breaks a hip. Many become nursing home residents, and depending on the study, up to 58 percent are dead within a year. This dwarfs breast cancer as a public health problem. Although hip fractures occur mainly in women, they can happen in men as well.

Hattie is 64 years old and works as a federal prosecutor. She is small, single, Chinese, and stressed. Her physician diagnosed her with "osteopenia" a decade ago. She treated Hattie in the office to a regimen of bisphosphonate injections and has followed her with dual-energy X-ray absorptiometry (DEXA) scans. But Hattie's scan scores have gotten worse. When she had a hip replaced, the orthopedic surgeon told her that the bone was "crumbly." Two years ago, Hattie began estrogen, selenium, DHEA, progesterone, vitamin K, testosterone pellets, and 10,000 IU of vitamin D. She recently started ipriflavone. Since beginning hormones, she can do jury trials and other high-intensity legal work like an attorney half her age. She was able to cut her Prozac dose in half. Her repeat DEXA showed that her bone density increased by 7 percent in two years. She is starting HGH and hopes to improve even more.

Physicians working with osteoporosis try first to eliminate causes such as steroids, smoking, and other drugs. After this, the pricey, FDA-approved bisphosphonate medications are usually tried. The industry promotes them for the prevention of bone thinning, but they are worse than nothing. They cause fractures, rotting jawbones, and even esophageal cancer. TheNNT.com summarizes the data, quoting a Cochrane meta-analysis. They say the drugs are ineffective for women without prior fractures and that they prevent bone breakage solely in the small group of women who have both osteoporosis on a scan plus a previously broken bone.

These facts make it hard to fathom why there are 80 million people using these drugs in the US. There is at least one good reason, however: our good doctors get about a 20 percent commission for dispensing medications like these in their offices. This is a terrific conflict of interest and would be criminal fee-splitting if physicians made a deal like this with another doctor instead of with a corporation. Another similar case is

Lupron, the chemical castration agent used for prostate cancer. You and your insurance company pay $10,000 for each shot, and the doctors get their cut of the loot. See the oncology section of *Butchered by "Healthcare"* for more.

Although the original studies claimed these drugs decrease bone breakage, this medication class *increases* fractures of the largest bone in the body, the femur. They also produce cases of irreversible jawbone rotting. Plaintiffs have filed thousands of lawsuits against Merck alleging their bisphosphonate, Fosamax, caused these disasters. The company paid $28 million to settle twelve hundred of them. These drugs also increase the risk of atrial fibrillation.

Most people hate this medication class because the drugs make them feel terrible. One website lists over 40 side effects. In contrast, hormone treatment makes most people feel wonderful along with preventing and reversing osteoporosis. DHEA, testosterone, vitamin D, and estrogen all have positive effects. HGH alone can improve bone density by eight percent a year.

Here are some non-hormonal treatments that are safe but more speculative. Selenium may help at a dose of one gram a day, increased after a month to two grams a day. Vitamin K2, one milligram per day, might also be valuable. Ipriflavone, 600 mg per day, is an approved prescription treatment for osteoporosis in Japan that is over-the-counter in the US. It may help if you already have the condition.

CHAPTER 18
"DOCTOR, I'M BLEEDING"

Women bleed after menopause for several reasons. During the "change of life," the year before they stop menstruating, most have a few last periods. I ask them to be patient and prescribe progesterone to shrink the uterine lining. With adequate doses, this works.

Even years after menopause, taking estrogen may stimulate the lining of the uterus to overgrow and bleed as it did in youth. The treatment for this is again progesterone. If these patients take enough, after a few months, their uterine lining shrinks and the bleeding stops.

Prolonged bleeding must be evaluated. "Trans-vaginal" ultrasounds are a non-invasive option that requires an instrument inserted into the vagina. If this shows that the uterine lining is thinner than 6 millimeters, uterine cancer is unlikely.

If malignancy is suspected, a biopsy must be done. There are two options. A small instrument may be inserted through the vagina into the uterus. Alternatively, a more complete scraping of the uterine interior called a "dilation and curettage" may be performed. The choice depends on circumstances, and the samples from either procedure are sent to a pathologist to see if there is cancer.

Early menopause bleeding: Women in their mid-40s to early 50s may have severe hot flashes and heavy, irregular menstrual periods. They may be anxious, bloated, depressed, and have low energy levels. This is the "peri-menopause." Estrogen levels stay high, but progesterone is usually low. Lab tests can confirm the diagnosis, but they are usually unnecessary. These women do not need estradiol yet, but progesterone helps control their symptoms.

How much progesterone is enough? One to eight 200 mg progesterone oral capsules a day for ten days or a bit longer will usually stop menopausal uterine bleeding if there is no other issue such as cancer. Alternatively, the progesterone troches may be used in the mouth, vagina, or rectum. These may not be as well absorbed. Patients become adjusted to the drug over a few weeks.

If progesterone does not work, the options to stop the bleeding include:

✪ Oral Provera 10 mg per day for ten days. This is much stronger than bio-identical progesterone.

✪ A single injection of bio-identical progesterone, 100 mg.

✪ Intravenous Premarin. This horse estrogen is more powerful than the human variety.

✪ Ovral birth control pills taken twice a day for several days. These are high-dose synthetic estrogen combined with a manufactured progestin.

✪ Surgical or cautery destruction (ablation) of the uterine interior.

✪ Mirena progestin intra-uterine device.

✪ Tranexamic acid (Lysteda) improves clotting but does not treat the underlying issue.

✪ Younger patients who are just beginning menopause are sometimes given a birth control pill such as Ortho-Novum 1/35 or Norinyl 1/35 to take continuously for 6-12 months. Note: this supplies contraception, but bio-identical drugs do not.

> **Sonia** is sixty-one, has been on hormone treatment, and had spotting like a mild menstrual period. I gave her oral progesterone and gradually increased her dose to 1000 mg a day. The drug made her sleepy at first, but her body adjusted after a few days and the bleeding stopped. She is getting a transvaginal ultrasound to make sure she has no build-up inside her uterus suggestive of cancer. Since Sonia had a dilation and curettage of her uterus two years ago that showed normal tissue, she did not need to go through that again.

Hormonal cycling: Many gynecologists believe that monthly withdrawal from hormones with an accompanying menstrual period is a good idea, even for seniors. But most women love the freedom of not having menses. Taking hormones shrinks the uterine lining and eventually controls bleeding. Using these medications every day of the month protects the brain, heart, bones, and breasts best.

Postscript: what is the most common cause of bleeding in a post-menopausal woman taking hormones? The traditional answer is to always think of uterine cancer. But the more likely cause is leaving town and forgetting to bring along the progesterone.

CHAPTER 19
BE CAREFUL WHOM YOU TRUST

We physicians do our best, but we make mistakes and have misconceptions. For example, many doctors who claim they practice anti-aging medicine use quantities or types of hormones that are ineffective. They learn about these from marketers selling them at conferences. Some prescribe less effective, outmoded drugs or generics of uneven quality.

You now know more about this field than most physicians. But everyone needs guidance, and even doctors should not write their own prescriptions. If you hear any of the following, be careful. The provider may not know what they are doing, or they might be putting their finances ahead of you.

~

SOME DOCTORS ARE MISINFORMED:
My doctor says I should age naturally, and that I should not take hormones. This is ridiculous. You should understand by now that the health benefits of supplementation are overwhelming.

My doctor told me I should stop my hormones. Another doctor said that the patch was the only safe estrogen. These ideas are nearly always wrong, but you have to be a "doctor whisperer" to understand why. Estrogen improves health more than any other hormone. Many of the beneficial effects of testosterone are because of its natural transformation into estrogen. These hormones are essential for everyone.

Patients may take natural estradiol in several ways, and there are advantages and disadvantages of each method:

METHOD:	DELIVERY:	ADVANTAGE:	DISADVANTAGE:
Patches	through skin	symptom relief	doesn't help heart
Creams	through skin	symptom relief	doesn't help heart
Premarin	oral	and helps heart	(rare) blood clots
Estradiol	oral	and helps heart	none

Patches deliver the drug through the skin and relieve menopausal symptoms. They are touted as safe because, unlike (oral) Premarin, they do not cause blood clots (deep vein thromboses or DVT). Oral estradiol does not cause clotting either, but many doctors refuse to prescribe it because they think that maybe all estrogens taken by mouth might cause blood clots just like Premarin does.

There is another health issue at stake. Both of the oral estrogens, estradiol and Premarin, protect against heart attacks by decreasing cholesterol buildup inside the coronary arteries. In contrast, transdermal estrogen—patches and creams—do not safeguard the heart the way the pills do.

The WHI study showed another tiny risk for one group of women taking Premarin. Those who were older than 65 had a slight increase in their heart disease risk—but only during the first year they took the drug. Every year after that, their chances of cardiac problems were lower than the group using no hormones. *So the overall heart benefits of Premarin proved to be far greater than the hazards.*

Confusions about this science have herded doctors into prescribing industry's profitable patches. Anti-aging groups have joined in and used these stories to promote their hormone creams. These, like the patch, have little risk, but unfortunately, they have no health benefits except symptom relief.

Since heart disease causes over half of all deaths, any drug that decreases this is indispensable. Women in the WHI who took Premarin for five years had forty percent fewer heart attack fatalities than those who took no medications. Subsequent studies using estradiol showed even higher benefits. *Effects like these dwarf the risks.*

Physicians live in a world of peer pressure, medical boards, and malpractice lawsuits. Calculations of risk versus reward are not always their focus or even a top priority. Most of them have heard something about the WHI study and fear getting blamed. So the following "standard of care" developed:

1) For older women or anyone with cardiac risk factors, some physicians prescribe only transdermal estrogen or even refuse to consider hormone replacement. These patients include the obese and those with a history of smoking, high blood pressure, diabetes, cholesterol, or a family history of heart disease—the people who need heart protection the most.

2) Women who are ten years or more after menopause are thought to benefit from hormones less and have higher risks. So they are also often only given the patch or even advised to stop estrogens altogether.

If estrogen is given through the skin—or worse, no replacement is prescribed—doctors do no harm. The outrage is that we do no good. Heart protection is far more important for frail, older patients than healthy, younger people.

My doctor says my levels are too high. This is often wrong. For most hormones, the upper limit of dosing and the highest appropriate blood levels are unknown or uncertain. Testosterone, vitamin D, and thyroid can be abused, but serious health issues are rare. See the Blood Testing and Dosing Guide in the appendix.

Key point: Blood levels are different depending on when they were checked. Immediately following the last dose, the level will be high. If blood is drawn just before the next dose is given, it will be lower. For consistency, check levels about five hours after a medication is taken.

Dosing decisions depend on age. Older people have bodies that are not as responsive as younger ones. For example, men in their thirties might have excellent sexual, intellectual, and muscular functioning with testosterone levels of only 650 ng/dl, but older men with this level might get deficiency symptoms. They might need 1200 ng/dl to feel and perform their best. Their cholesterol often stays elevated unless their testosterone is pushed well over 1000 ng/dl.

Some bodybuilders who take testosterone have risky cholesterol numbers, and steroids have a reputation for causing heart disease. But many of these guys—they are mostly men—use ten times the replacement dose of testosterone or more.

Vitamin D is almost completely safe if 10,000 IU a day or less is taken. People under 200 pounds might start with 5000 IU. Checking blood levels should be a routine medical practice, and they usually show that more is needed. The goal is the higher end of 60-100 ng/ml. Vitamin D toxicity typically requires consuming massive doses and levels around 300. Of course, if this is suspected, the supplement must be stopped.

Thyroid: Recall that in Grave's disease abnormal antibodies stimulate the thyroid gland to go wild and produce massive amounts of the hormone. The only way to control the blood level in that situation is to use other drugs. By the time these are effective, patients can be in trouble. This syndrome can cause osteoporosis and atrial fibrillation.

Patients who take thyroid hormone for a hypothyroid condition have negligible risks. If they use too much, they get uncomfortable warning signs such as nervousness. This happens before harm is done, so the drug can be reduced or temporarily discontinued. There are rare exceptions, so a physician's care is helpful.

Mainstream doctors who have experience with Grave's have seen all this, so they are cautious. They may recommend doses that are too conservative for optimal health and wellbeing. Hormone doctors (in theory) carefully observe the patients' responses and sometimes increase the medication until the T3 and T4 tests are in their lab's high-normal range. Review the thyroid sections and see Appendix A for more.

*"I am very cautious about committing someone to medication for life."** The author is right—there is reason for concern. But if you hear this from a physician, remember that most of them spend their careers promiscuously prescribing pills for cholesterol, diabetes, hypertension, and even "attention-deficit hyperactivity disorder" (ADHD)—all to be taken lifelong. Most of them believe SSRIs such as Prozac work for depression "just like insulin works for diabetes" (*Butchered by Healthcare* has more about antidepressants). But lifestyle improvements could replace nearly all of these medications.

Human hormones are identical or nearly identical to body components. *Raising their levels to those of youth is precisely the same as using insulin, which is another bio-identical hormone.* This is a fact, not an analogy. These are not toxic chemicals with unnatural side effects, and when prescribed properly, their benefits are far greater than their risks.

*Dr. Kathleen L. Wyne, who serves on the Sex Hormone and Reproductive Endocrinology Scientific Committee for the American Association of Clinical Endocrinologists.

My doctor told me I should quit my hormones because of the "black boxes." The FDA places these worrisome warnings on the product information label after the drug is already on the market. For example, in 2003, the year after the WHI was published, they put a black box on products containing estrogen and progesterone. This claimed these hormones caused an increase in the risk of stroke, breast cancer, heart disease, and myocardial infarction. And in 2015, they put a black box on testosterone saying it caused strokes and heart attacks. These warnings are supposed to help consumers and doctors, but for bio-identical hormones, with rare exceptions, they are wrong—you have seen the evidence.

The FDA warns about other hormones as well. For example, they said HGH causes cancer, but only a few case reports in the entire literature suggest this. Other studies show no link between HGH and cancer. HGH inhibits prostate cancer.

These advisories seem solely designed to protect the FDA. Since patients are being damaged—and dying—this is criminal negligence. Ignorance of the literature should be no defense. See the FDA chapter of Butchered by "Healthcare" in the bonus section to learn how the FDA gets away with this behavior.

∾

OTHER DOCTORS ARE AFTER YOUR MONEY:

My doctor gives me a special cream combination made just for me. **Or:** *My doctor says the best thing for me is to get a shot every three weeks that they formulate especially for me.*

Even going into a doctor's office for a testosterone pellet is a small conflict of interest. The doctor gets paid to insert it and is motivated by that rather than being strictly concerned about your health. Physicians must never own drugstores, nor should they manufacture or sell medications in their offices. Activities like these have a prejudicial effect on their judgment—they might be tempted to give you the most expensive and profitable thing instead of putting your interests first. Doctors should instead recommend quality pharmacies that have choices and are reasonably priced.

Go to the lab/X-ray center/MRI in my office. Ditto. If your doctor has *any financial relationship* with a pharmacy, vitamin sales, medical imaging center, or other medical business, these conflicts of interest affect their judgment. Disclosure is not good enough—consider seeing someone else.

My provider is checking my saliva, so I don't need blood tests. Salivary levels only correlate with blood levels before patients ever take medications. They are unreliable after drugs are given, *so they should not be used to monitor therapy.* Unlicensed practitioners such as nutritionists and chiropractors can retail salivary testing, so they promote and profit from it. Mainstream doctors from physician associations including NAMS, ACOG, and AACE deny its usefulness, and in this case, they are right. This controversy confuses the hormone debate, undermines the doctors who are doing proper care, and decreases hormone replacement credibility.

My pharmacist and my nutritionist say prescriptions are too strong for me and recommend that I take their gentle over-the-counter medicines made from plants. These have few or no active ingredients, so they do not work. Blood (forget salivary) testing proves this. The doctors are confused, so why would you listen to what a druggist or nutritionist says about a product that they profit from?

CHAPTER 20
FREQUENTLY ASKED QUESTIONS

How long should I take replacement? Is it OK to stop when I get old? You can do whatever you want. But if you want to feel and look your best and continue to be protected from many diseases, do not stop. People who quit supplementation will soon feel the same as they did before. They also will have the same risks as before of various diseases. For example, pain with sex and other vaginal problems may return. Osteoporosis and the risk of fractures increase.

Since progesterone relaxes women, should men who are anxious and have insomnia take it as well? No. Men should never take progesterone because it injures their health. It makes them fat, increases inflammation, and decreases their sexual interest. When a progestin-type synthetic progesterone was studied for male birth control, the trial was stopped early because of unacceptable health effects such as these.

Progestins have been used on male sex offenders in prison populations to suppress sexuality. But for normal men, a robust interest in sex is a measure of good health.

The goal for hormone replacement should be to mimic the blood levels of youth. Young men have progesterone blood levels of only about .2 ng/ml. Since progesterone in men is naturally so low, supplementation is unlikely to be good for them. In contrast, women have levels during the second phase of their menstrual cycles of 10-20 ng/ml. This is their treatment goal.

Are male testosterone levels falling in the entire population? Yes. A study of 4045 American men between 1999 and 2016 showed that their testosterone was declining. The average level dropped from over 600 ng/dl at the beginning of the study to the mid-400s at the end. And in 1999, only four percent had grossly deficient levels (under 300 ng/dl). By 2016, 21 percent had numbers this low. Another study published in 2006 showed that 39 percent of US men over 45 years old were testosterone deficient. No one knows for sure what caused this trend. It could relate to diet, toxins, exercise, obesity, or marijuana.

Jared was only 36 when he first saw his hormone doctor: *I had read about testosterone supplementation for several years and started to wonder. I am an accountant and work sixty to seventy hours a week and initially thought I was just fatigued. I was working out an hour and a half a day, and my body just never seemed to respond. My wife had left me for nine months last year because she wanted more sex than I did. Even when she came back, we still weren't getting along because I couldn't perform. My doctor put it all together for me. My T levels were only 180 ng/dl. And he thought I likely had minimal brain damage because I played a lot of soccer as a kid and had headed the ball so many times. When I started testosterone injections, I began feeling better almost immediately. Although things aren't perfect, my wife has been much less demanding since I have been taking care of her better sexually. My doctor gave me Viagra for a few months, but I gave it away to one of my gym buddies. I don't need it anymore.*

Sperm counts are declining at about the same rate as testosterone for both younger and older men. And erectile dysfunction (ED) is frequently diagnosed, even in younger age groups. Perhaps normal people are labeling themselves with this because they watch too much pharmaceutical TV advertising.

According to hormone specialist Sean Breen, the most common cause of low testosterone levels in younger men is head trauma. Modern football helmets cause more concussions rather than fewer concussions because they allow competitors to use their heads as impact weapons against other players. "Heading" the ball in soccer may cause brain injury as well. A related issue is that veterans can suffer brain damage during their service. It is poorly recognized, and many need help.

Repetitive impacts may injure the brain's frontal lobes, and this leads to more aggressive behavior. Because many sports demand combat-type skills, players with this damage may function better in competition. This creates a vicious cycle of more sports success, more trauma, then further injury.

Professional athletes are the most affected. Aaron Hernandez played football since youth, murdered a friend, and finally killed himself. His autopsy revealed severe brain damage.

Some young athletes take substantial amounts of testosterone during their playing years, and it makes a few aggressive. This is rare with conventional doses. Older men often say testosterone makes them feel calmer and more confident.

I have genes that make me five times more likely to get breast cancer and fifteen times more likely to get ovarian cancer (BRCA-1 and 2). Should I still take estrogen after menopause?

BRCA-positive women are usually told to get castrated. This substantially decreases their risk of breast cancer and of course has wondrous effects for future ovarian cancer. Lowered estrogen levels were thought to be the reason for the decrease in breast cancer. So the oncologists naturally concluded that giving these women estrogen would be risky. This turned out to be wrong.

When supplemental estrogen was studied in these patients, the risk of breast cancer was about half of what it was if estrogen was not taken. Even with a family history of breast cancer, studies showed no increase in breast cancer if estrogen is taken. It has a protective effect.

Do hormones allow you to live longer? Various physician associations claim their treatments are "anti-aging." Older people with higher levels of HGH, estrogen, and testosterone look healthy. We have studies comparing patients who use hormones to those who do not, and the treated patients have better health. However, scientific proof for longevity would require watching large groups until many of them die. This is easy to do with mice but hard to do with humans.

Are these medications a treatment or a preventive? As a general rule, prevention works better than attempting a cure after a disease has taken root. For example, estrogen therapy reduces Alzheimer's risks, but after the disease advances, it is less help. Patients taking progesterone have lower rates of breast and uterine cancers, a preventive measure.

Even after people have bone thinning, supplementation with HGH and testosterone increases density. So prevention and treatment both work for osteoporosis. Reversal of other conditions such as heart disease may be possible. Testosterone has been used to treat breast cancer, and estrogen suppresses advanced prostate cancer.

What about the horses used to produce Premarin? Animal activists are trying to protect the miserable pregnant Canadian horses that supply urine for Premarin. They (the horses, not the activists) have strap-on catheters, which cause equine health problems and lead to premature death. Some Premarin products are now synthesized from soy. Some are also made from yams, but their quality is not as good.

Why am I still seeing Prempro ads on TV in 2021? Premarin and Provera's sales peaked at about $2 billion in 2002. By 2006, sales were down to $1 billion, and Prempro, the combination drug, went off patent in 2015. Pfizer was still promoting it with extravagant TV advertising in 2020. Prempro must have still been profitable despite their expenditure of $330 million to settle 2,200 Provera breast cancer lawsuits that year.

Should hormones be prescribed before surgery? Deficiencies of vitamins such as C and zinc are a cause of poor healing. So many doctors recommend supplements before operations.

Certain hormones are "anabolic," which means they promote growth, build tissue, and improve healing. Testosterone, other anabolic steroids, and human growth hormone can treat muscle loss and wasting syndromes such as AIDS.

Before doing an operation, I always discussed hormone deficiency symptoms with my patients. If they had any, I offered treatment. I believe that hormone preparation should be routine, but mainstream surgeons do not do this.

Sam's text: *Hi, I wanted to tell you I work out with a trainer and have gained muscle and lost 15 pounds. I have been on the medicines for about a year now, and I started working out eight months ago. Thank you for changing my life for the better.*

What exercise should I do while using hormones? For best results, easy weightlifting is required! Use the machines at the gym for a minimum of a half-hour twice a week. This is enough unless you have a special interest. For either sex, your results will be more rapid if you take testosterone.

Start with one set of eight to ten repetitions using ten to fifteen machines. This is easy to learn, but get some advice if you are new to it. Try to use muscles from every part of your body during each workout. Splitting your routine between body parts on different days is only necessary if you get serious.

Lift light weights at first. Do not worry about getting big—it does not happen with this sort of program. The machines are designed for safety and rarely cause injury. You will get firmer and see improvement within a month. Woody Allen's saying applies here: "Ninety percent of success is just showing up." You will also get a broad sense of optimism after your workouts, no matter how you felt before.

I had a 75-year-old friend who was so deconditioned that he had trouble walking up and down stairs. I took him to a gym and coached him for two hours. He stuck with my program twice a week for years. I never worked with him again, and he never took testosterone. He is 88 now, his posture is excellent, and he can do whatever he wants. He boasts about feeling good, being powerful, and enjoying dancing at his club.

Yoga is virtually a sacrament in Los Angeles where I live. If you have back, shoulder, or neck pain, these will improve within a month or two after starting practice. Hands-on instruction is helpful for six to twelve months. The teachers get tiresome, but I like Baron Baptiste. One of his book reviewers said that a half-hour daily of this workout put him in the best shape of his life.

"A spiritual master driving the yoga revolution." —*Self*

JOURNEY INTO POWER

How to Sculpt Your Ideal Body, Free Your True Self, and Transform Your Life with Yoga

BARON BAPTISTE

NEW YORK TIMES BESTSELLING AUTHOR OF *PERFECTLY IMPERFECT*

Recommended yoga text.

"Flow" and "hot" yoga are both challenging. Bikram is one of the most demanding. It is a cult—I know because I was a card-carrying member for eight years. The heat in the rooms has crept up every decade, and now may be above 110 degrees. This is too hot. Some instructors discourage drinking water during the workout, which is crazy. Students occasionally pass out with heat exhaustion, are dragged out of the studio, and rushed to the emergency room.

Once you understand yoga basics, you can use online classes. Practicing thirty to forty minutes three days a week is all you need to become durable, flexible, and have great posture. If you do yoga at home, you will have no parking trouble and not have to put up with other sweaty students. And you will not have to listen to the idiocy about backbends curing cancer. You might even violate a few rules if yoga is not your religion—you can wear shoes, use weights, and listen to podcasts or music.

The author in 2018 doing yoga with weights.

The next step, if you are interested, is to find a sport you enjoy.

I liked to climb, but I am too old for it now.

Massage can help your mobility, especially deep-tissue. Consider taking Advil and Tylenol before you go so you can tell your masseuse to be aggressive.

PART VI
EVERYONE WANTS YOUR MONEY

CHAPTER 21
THE HORMONE MARKETING CIRCUS

The trouble with the world is that the stupid are cocksure and the intelligent full of doubt.

— BERTRAND RUSSELL

Hormone therapy has many benefits. Because of claims that it does harm, I must introduce you to the people with their hands in the till.

PHARMACEUTICAL COMPANIES ARE THE MAIN FINANCIAL SUPPORT for physicians' organizations. Medical societies routinely confess that they are "funded by an unrestricted grant from company x." Free money is fiction, of course. Those who supply funding demand their due or they will quit paying. Besides these millions of dollars, Pharma gives other "freebies" including trinkets, research money, fees for speakers, fees for exhibitors, complimentary ghostwriting, and support for various kinds of publications.

Industry's closest observers believe that since federal law has restricted money and gifts given to individual physicians, Pharma's focus has shifted to changing practice standards by influencing prominent doctors. The companies spend 20 percent of their vast marketing budget on these "key opinion leaders," and they even have an acronym, KOLs. Many get $500,000 to $1 million or more a year in grants and for study support. This concealed ransom is harder to track and has a more pernicious influence than advertising.

The recipients of gifts like these claim their conflicts-of-interest disclosures sanitize these relationships. And every physician society has a policy statement stating that they have no commercial bias. Their leaders protest their objectivity in journals. (See Jerome Kassirer's *On the Take,* 2004).

These physician groups churn out hundreds of "standard of practice" statements. Industry advertising agencies spin even a lukewarm endorsement into revenue, and observers have criticized this practice for decades. A study in JAMA entitled "Are the Guidelines Following the Guidelines?" (1999) said that these rules are far from true standards of care. In 2000, Roberto Grilli and his colleagues published a *Lancet* article describing 431 such statements. Eighty-eight percent lacked disclaimers or relevant literature references. The bulk of the authors had conflicts of interest.

Other studies agreed: physician guidelines are deceptive and almost useless. One review found that four out of five contributors to these standards are paid by corporations. Each author had an average of ten conflicts of interest. But physician policy statements like these have the weight of expert testimony in court.

Why do most physicians refuse to prescribe hormones?
Physician trade associations and the FDA obey the Pharma

companies. These all encourage patent drug prescribing and oppose bio-identicals. The Health Maintenance Organizations (HMOs) and Preferred Provider Organizations (PPOs) monitor doctors who use drugs that are outside the "standards." If they step out of line, they may get fired or have their contracts revoked. Doctors are afraid.

An example: many cardiologists body-build and use injectable testosterone. Many understand it is safe, decreases heart disease, and improves depression. But for their patients, they continue writing prescriptions for antidepressants and statin cholesterol medicines as their protocols command. Few of them offer hormone treatments.

Here is how the physician groups cooperate with big Pharma. The American Association of Clinical Endocrinologists (AACE) has a 2017 guideline for treating menopause. By the time it was written, they had well over a decade to examine the Women's Health Initiative (WHI) and the follow-up studies. Here are a few of their conclusions:

> *When the use of progesterone is* necessary, (my emphasis) *micronized progesterone is considered the safer alternative... Newer information supports the previous recommendation against the use of bio-identical hormones... The publication of the Women's Health Initiative (WHI) in 2002... found a negative impact of HRT* [hormone replacement therapy] *on cardiovascular risk in postmenopausal women, while finding a small increase in relative risk of breast cancer in women treated with estrogen/progesterone combination, but not with estrogen alone.*

They dislike the bio-identicals, yet they recommend bio-identical progesterone, when "necessary." This refers to their bizarre stance that progesterone in any form is undesirable after a hysterectomy. They also seem not to have understood that the WHI did not apply to human substances. The last line is accurate, but they couldn't quite say it: synthetic Provera—not human progesterone—causes breast cancer, but Premarin does not. They should have added that Premarin improves cardiovascular risks but causes a few blood clots and that soon after the WHI was published, further studies proved that bio-identical estradiol was nearly harmless.

AACE has 29 "corporate partners" including Pfizer and Roche. The head author of the 2011 menopause guidelines, Goodman, disclosed payment by Bayer, Noven, and Pfizer. The doctors who wrote these standards were brilliant intellectual academic physicians. They must have understood the hormone issues but had to answer to their donors.

Many AACE endocrinologists quit in 2016 because they felt the organization was covering up the critical story about T3. To get their members back, AACE softened their guidelines. Instead of solely recommending T4 as before, they said T3 was an acceptable alternative.

The AACE recently shut its state chapters because of internal dissent. Many of their members were using porcine thyroid, and some questioned the utility of TSH. They may have been primarily concerned that their patients were defecting to thyroid "wellness" clinics that were getting better results. In response, the Texas endocrinologists formed an independent chapter.

Another association, the North American Menopause Society (NAMS) said:

> Treatment of moderate to severe vasomotor symptoms (hot flashes) is the primary indication for hormone therapy… Progestogen therapy (progesterone and synthetic progestogens) is an option to treat hot flashes…

They did not acknowledge the decade-old literature about the bio-identical drugs' health benefits or point out the diseases caused by imitation progesterone. NAMS has many drug company donors. These include Pfizer, Amgen, Allergan, Ascend Therapeutics, EndoCeutics, Inc., Exeltis USA, Pharmavite LLC, Radius Health, Reckitt Benckiser, Sebela Pharmaceuticals Inc., Shinogi Inc., and Therapeutics MD.

The American Congress of Obstetricians and Gynecologists (ACOG) is a fellow traveler. They echo these themes: "In general, hormone therapy use should be limited to the treatment of menopausal symptoms at the lowest dose for the shortest amount of time possible."

NAMS, AACE, and ACOG all have extensive financial links to Pfizer (formerly Wyeth), which makes Prempro. By 2012, this company had about $1.2 billion in plaintiff's settlements and verdicts related to the WHI. But paying these required only a fraction of Pfizer's revenues, so they could still afford to support doctors.

In 2017, the FDA approved a proprietary oral bio-identical estrogen/progesterone combination in four different doses. Although the quality is likely excellent, dosage adjustment and price issues remain. ACOG and NAMS support it. They say it uses bio-identical hormones of FDA-approved products as opposed to the "unregulated and not approved hormones made by compounding pharmacies." Interpretation: they are right: we cannot completely trust compounded or generic medications— nor can we always be sure patients are taking their pills. So we check levels. At least with human drugs, cancer and blood clots are of little concern.

My recommendation is to ignore these guilds and its guidelines. Influence theory says that substantial gifts have overwhelming effects on behavior. Since big Pharma donates millions of dollars each year to these societies, we can assume that their standards reflect the economic interests of their patrons.

OTHER ACTS IN THIS CARNIVAL

A physician friend called the alternative medicine hormone

scene "the quacks selling to the wackos." There is some truth to this, but the standard medicine described above is far worse. They use the full weight and authority of healthcare to discredit bio-identical therapy and promote problematic patent drugs including counterfeit hormones.

⊙ **The American Academy of Anti-Aging Medicine (A4M.com)** is more right than wrong. Science and experience support most of their ideas. They are a successful nonprofit with 26,000 members and the most credible large hormone society.

The A4M, like any physician association, has many corporate supporters. ZRT labs, which sells questionable salivary tests, is one of their sponsors and pays doctors to lecture to the membership about their products. And the Academy is linked to promoters of ineffective cream progesterone.

At the A4M meetings, exhibit halls are full of people hawking magic crystals, foot massagers, and supplements with pseudoscientific names. I once heard one of their speakers claim that progesterone protects the prostate gland. This is incorrect— when men take progesterone, their chances of vascular disease, cholesterol deposition, and arterial plaque rupture increase. These are inflammatory and cause heart attacks.

⊙ **Teresa Wiley**, who has no traditional healthcare credentials, invented the Wiley Protocol. She markets cream hormones in trademarked, patent-protected combinations. Her formulas blend thyroid, estrogen, progesterone, DHEA, and testosterone. Their composition varies by the day of the month and the time of the year. The Wiley Protocol avoids shots, most pills, injectable pellets, and patented transdermal patches.

During certain days of the month, her creams have no or few active ingredients. This withdrawal causes menstrual periods for some women. Domestic partners cycle alongside them. For example, higher doses of testosterone are used for both people during certain periods of the month in an attempt to match their sexual interests.

Comment: Wiley's program is a clever promotion of bio-identicals but not the best option. The biggest challenge in hormone therapy is getting patients to use enough medication. Those who receive less are more vulnerable to cancer, heart disease, Alzheimer's, and other conditions. Cycling and using cream preparations create lower blood levels on average than pills or other delivery systems. The Wiley patients are also instructed to use her products up to three times a day. Few patients can manage this.

I view myself as a coach rather than a purveyor of special formulas. I use a variety of compounders to avoid most of the expensive patented drugs. The medicines my patients take are convenient, versatile, and reasonably priced. I educate patients about all options and we see what works best for each one.

✪ **Suzanne Somers** has star power. Millions of TV viewers follow and believe in her. Her promotion of human hormones transformed many women's lives and refuted many of Pharma's unhealthy but profitable fictions. She is a user and popularizer of the Wiley Protocol.

Sommers is an advocate of estriol, the bio-identical but weak estrogen that might increase the chances of breast cancer. Recall also that progesterone protects against breast cancer, and that creams and cycling potentially deliver less total hormone than the oral micronized or troche types taken daily. (Even these may not produce optimal blood levels for progesterone.) It may or may not be coincidental that Somers developed breast cancer a few years ago.

✪ **Christine Northup, MD,** is the author of *The Wisdom of Menopause*. She is a traditionally trained gynecologist who has either sold out or believes in mysticism. Northrup touts Tarot cards, astrology, angels, and all kinds of supplements. She thinks menopause is a good time to be a social justice warrior and has been on Oprah several times.

✪ **Worldlinkmedical,** the Academy of Preventive and Innovative Medicine (worldlinkmedical.com), is the "straight man" of these groups. It was started by Neal Rousier, MD, to promote physician education and patient training. They have videos and articles for patients and physicians. Their doctors can attend seminars, join their professional organization, and participate in the forum. Neal has an international following and spends months each year training foreign physicians in their home countries.

Worldlinkmedical has no commercial bias that I could find, and although the organization makes a living for its administrator, the big money flows elsewhere. I trained with them, so their views are the closest to my own. If you want to learn more, this is the place to start.

✪ **Unconventional healthcare providers** often claim they have a place at this table. They treat hormone deficiencies with over-the-counter products that have few or no active ingredients. Ben Goldacre gave me the best way to think about them:

> *Alternative therapists who sell vitamins and homeopathy sugar pills, which perform no better than placebo in fair tests, have no role to play. These business people often like to pretend, with an affectation of outside swagger, that their trade somehow challenges the pharmaceutical industry. In reality, they are cut from the same cloth, and simply use cruder versions of the same tricks. Problems in medicine do not mean that homeopathic sugar pills work; just because there are problems with aircraft design, that doesn't mean that magic carpets really fly.*

> — *BAD PHARMA* (2012)

Counterpoint: Although bad advice is everywhere, frauds, sellouts, and business people are not the entirety of healthcare. Nobility remains, and doctors often perform miracles.

CHAPTER 22
THREE GOLIATHS VS DAVID

Big Pharma and their financially captive FDA are trying to squeeze the compounders out of business. If they succeed, hormone treatments will be less versatile and effective.

COMPOUNDERS WERE THE FIRST PHARMACISTS, AND THEY HAVE A venerable tradition spanning millennia. For example, compounding pharmacies developed a drug to treat malaria made from tree bark. In 1877, Dr. Squib, a compounding pharmacist, created standards for US medications and later started his eponymous company. Other drugmakers founded Merck, Sandoz, Upjohn, and Eli Lilly. These companies made drugs for individual patients, but later developed into massive operations churning out manufactured medications. As late as the 1960s, most drugs were still being compounded, but this practice has declined to less than five percent today.

The pharmaceutical companies obtain new medicines either by inventing them or buying them from competitors or government-funded developers. The drugmakers are also allowed to patent certain bio-identicals based on proprietary delivery systems such as transdermal patches. Strangely, they have also been permitted to patent and assume control of specific doses and combinations of human hormones. There is nothing special about these except the branding and the marketing—compounders can easily manufacture them. Examples include certain estradiol-progesterone combinations and the Prometrium natural brand of progesterone patented for 100 and 200 mg. AndroGel is a branded bio-identical testosterone gel for men, patented at 1 and 1.62 percent.

When a doctor writes a prescription for a compounding pharmacy, under the current rules she must claim her patients need something unique that is not supplied by the big drugmakers. These include drug combinations or doses that are at least 20 percent higher or lower than the ones the industry has available. Examples of compounded drugs include:

✪ 300 mg progesterone capsules. The patented ones are 100 and 200 mg.

✪ Testosterone creams of 10 and 20 percent, much higher than AndroGel.

✪ The weak bio-identical estrogens, estrone, and estriol are sometimes combined with estradiol. This is an excuse to compound—the mix works no better than estradiol alone.

If a patented drug is available, reasonably priced, and appropriate, it would be the top choice. But this never happens because brand names are outrageously expensive. Sometimes, however, economical patented drugs under a different name but made by the same companies can be found abroad. Patients can either travel there or buy from websites.

Big Pharma has gouged US consumers so thoroughly that 90 percent of the medications purchased here are generic. These are often adequate, but consumers may receive a different product each time they reorder. The reason? Wholesale pharmacies are always searching the international markets for the lowest-priced product to dump on retailers. No one notices the switch until the patient takes the drug. Many people who have found stability using one generic have problems with a new one. Side effects may appear, the potency may be different, or the drug may even be ineffective. I have seen this with Norvasc, Synthroid, and Toprol XL generics.

Compounders' medications are usually of excellent quality and reasonably priced. Their system makes individualizing doses and formulations convenient. They are currently the best choice for most bio-identical hormones.

One downside of compounding is that the law requires short expiration dates for these drugs. This makes compounded drugs less competitive than patented ones because if patients do not use their prescription right away, they have to buy them again. The huge companies may have influenced the development of this regulation to harass their tiny competitors. But the compounders benefit from repeat purchases as well. There is no practical reason for these rules—a pharmacist confided to me they make their medications from materials that have at least a two-year shelf-life.

Note: Individual state's pharmacy boards, not the FDA, supervise the compounders, and the Pharmacy Compounding Accreditation Board (PCAB) certifies them. If your druggist isn't on these lists, they may have quality issues.

Big Pharma, abetted by their captive physician groups and the FDA, is trying to run US compounders out of business—three Goliaths against a David. An article in *Menopause* (2016) describes the conspiracy:

> *The Endocrine Society, The North American Menopause Society, American Congress of Obstetricians and Gynecologists, American Society for Reproductive Medicine, and International Menopause Society recommend against CBHT* [compounded bio-identical

hormone therapy] *use by anyone without a medical condition*
preventing them from using FDA-approved HT [hormone therapy].
The FDA has issued a caution against compounded drug use. Their
concerns include inadequate evidence of efficacy and safety, variable
purity and potency, and insufficient labeling.

The paper sounds authoritative and has 87 references. But
these physician organizations are deep inside industry's pock-
ets. Each author of this statement gets money from more than 5
mega-companies. They also used "medical writing support,"
which may mean that corporate ghostwriters wrote the whole
thing. These are conflicts of interest, the politically correct way
to describe money changing hands.

Drugmakers have repeatedly lied to us and they have
committed more felonies than any industry in history, as judged
by their criminal settlements. They have their own Wikipedia
page of shame about it. We hold out their patent drugs as
paragons, but they are not. My other book describes many
related issues. For example, the following products had to be
recalled:

✪ Bayer's Cutter Laboratories' blood products with HIV in
them. Instead of destroying the inventory, they sold it to Asian
and Latin American markets without heat treating it to reduce
the risk. Many hemophiliacs who received it tested newly positive for HIV and some developed AIDS.

✪ Many patent medications including Ketorolac contaminated with particulate matter, rubbing alcohol contaminated
with the toxic alcohol methanol, and drugs containing a
carcinogen called nitrosamine.

✪ Birth control pills with labeling mistakes that could have
resulted in pregnancy.

✪ Several drugs with toxic preservatives that were not listed
on the label.

INDUSTRY'S LATEST SALVO IN THE WAR ON COMPOUNDERS IS THE 2020 publication of The Clinical Utility of Compounded Bio-identical Hormone Therapy: A Review of Safety, Effectiveness, and Use. This is an aggressive attack on a system that has provided us with safe drugs for more than a century. The authors recommend massive federal regulation, including using the FDA to oversee compounders. They also propose categorizing most currently compounded medications as "difficult to compound," which would virtually eliminate them. If these suggestions are implemented, it would be the end of doctors' autonomy to provide specified, quality drugs for individual patients. Luckily, these proposals have generated pushback from 32 members of Congress, who signed a letter opposing them.

The FDA paid the National Academy of Sciences to write this review. Since more than half the Agency's budget comes from Pharma, the National Academy—a supposedly neutral organization—has allowed itself to become a stalking horse for drug corporations. Each of these players understands the true golden rule—those with the gold make the rules.

If you want to help, see the Alliance for Pharmacy Compounding (a4pc.org) and savemycompounds.com. The National Community Pharmacists Association (NCPA) (https://ncpa.org/) is another firm supporter of compounding. A third organization to contact is the American Pharmacists Association (APhA) (https://pharmacist.com/).

The medical industry versus patients.

CHAPTER 23
CONCLUSION

Do you want to live a long life? There are no guarantees, but your chances of staying healthy are better if you supplement your hormones as you age. The bio-identicals decrease menopause and andropause symptoms. They also strengthen health, intellect, sexuality, and physical performance. Keeping your levels youthful also lowers your chances of heart disease, diabetes, Alzheimer's, many cancers, and other medical problems. These medications could be more beneficial than exercise and are possibly as important as diet.

Our physicians, corporations, and regulatory bodies claim the "standard-of-care" is to use these natural substances sparingly and in low doses. Who benefits from this swindle? The patent drug owners, of course. We gave them our public healthcare money, they have been calling the shots, and they are gouging us.

For doctors: Regardless of your original training, familiarizing yourself with hormone therapy using lectures and reference materials will enhance your patient care. The distortions

you have read about here introduce *Butchered by "Healthcare."*
Reading this will make you still more skeptical about medical
studies and accepted practices. "Evidence-based medicine" is a
commercialized mess.

For patients: No matter your sex, have your hormones
checked if you are depressed, anxious, or fatigued. PMS,
menopause, or low testosterone may be the cause. Never
assume that you have overwhelming situational or philosoph-
ical issues and that you are beaten. Human beings function
smoothly and maintain optimism despite enormous stresses—
but if you have a hormone deficiency, psychological illnesses are
near-universal. And beware of antidepressants or other psych
medications. These are more likely to injure mental health than
to heal it.

All this is controversial, so you must study these matters and
take them into your own hands. Certainly, avoid the chemical
and animal imitation hormones devised by the corporations.
Premarin and its relatives slightly increase the risk of blood
clots, and the progestins such as Provera cause a few breast
cancer deaths. Whenever possible, steer clear of other synthetic
drugs because their risks are often higher than their benefits.

As to your relationship with physicians: some are wonderful,
many are frustrating, and of course, all have human flaws. View
them as your servants. Never tolerate a condescending attitude
and do not put anyone on a pedestal. If you do the homework,
you might learn more about a medical subject than most
doctors. But healthcare is complicated, and the right provider
offers a lot. Always pursue collaboration and courteous relationships.

You can forget everything else here if you remember you
deserve to feel great. If your practitioner or therapy does not
help you, move on. American healthcare has over a million
physicians, and you should not have doubts about yours. For a

few hundred dollars, you can have a virtual consultation with almost anyone. You may find a mentor, an advocate, or even a friend. Although we are beset from every side, do not count doctors out—most of us have a heart of idealism still.

CHAPTER 24
HOW TO FIND CARE

Maria is 60. She has never worked, but she tried to take care of herself. She always put her kids and family before her own needs. Two years ago, Maria's husband died in bed beside her after he lost his long fight with cancer. Since then, Maria has tried to focus on herself. Her menopause symptoms were mild, but I offered her hormone therapy and she tried it. With vitamin D, progesterone, estrogen, thyroid, and testosterone pellets, Maria has transformed. She now goes salsa dancing three times a week and has several boyfriends. After weight loss, breast implants, and a little liposuction, Maria looks like a forty-year-old. Lab tests showed the best cholesterol numbers of her life.

Well-trained providers can be found at worldlinkmedical.com. For example, Sean Breen, MD, (doctorbreen.com) is in Los Angeles. I am less familiar with the American Academy of Anti Aging Medicine (A4M.com), but they have a huge membership. You can find a nearby provider by searching their member directory.

Many nurse practitioners do a great job and may be more empathetic and economical than a physician. They practice independently in some states. Robert L. Morgan, APRN, (Kingwoodwellness.com, Houston) was a sought-after provider who authored the weight loss chapter. He charged $150 for the first visit and another $150 for a laboratory blood panel and did virtual consultations. His people have qualified replacements who he trained.

The physicians at palmspringsbioidenticalhormones.com take care of hormones and leave the other medical care to primary care doctors. They charge about $1000 in the first year. Labs and medicines are extra, but their blood panel is only $100. In subsequent years, their fee is less. They check lab tests every 12 months to see how you are doing.

I interviewed one of the Cenegenics.com physicians several years ago. He said that his clinic charged about $30,000 a year for its premium anti-aging program. The package included testing, follow-up, medications, and workout supervision. He said their doctors saw only one or two patients a day. The only issue I found was that they were using estrogen blockers. Their website has "after treatment" photos of senior men with six-pack abdominal muscles and busty women (this link was accessed using the Wayback Machine internet archive; their current website is more modest).

If you call Cenegenics, a salesperson will make sure you can afford them. Then you will speak to one of their physicians. My source told me that the clinic was giving their doctors $1000 for every patient they persuaded to sign up.

Other doctors claim they specialize in "functional" medicine and have "concierge" practices. This typically includes a lot of personal services. These physicians claim they examine each patient's background, nutrition, and environment instead of just looking at isolated symptoms. Their charges are sometimes $2000 a year or more, not including testing and drugs. Some use

TV, radio, or even billboard marketing. Patients may defect from one of these high-priced situations after they figure out the medications and doses they need.

Hormone care belongs in the hands of primary care physicians, but they have a hard time doing this work along with everything else. They are up to their necks in a quagmire of insurance, regulation, administration, documentation, and the responsibilities of general patient care. Many of their peers and most specialists are against hormone therapy, so general doctors often get intimidated.

Hormone science is hard to grasp and the politics are hard to believe. Physicians do this work because we hope to help our patients and make some money along the way. But creating a profitable hormone practice is difficult, and few of us are comfortable marketing our services. And the doctors who hold corporate contracts must abide by rigid protocols. In some situations, these seem to be a bigger priority than patient wellbeing.

Patients pay their insurance companies outrageous premiums and assume they should not have to pay more for us. But if hormone doctors bill insurers, they often ask for a "letter of necessity." If we write one, their reviewers may tell the state medical board we are not practicing the standard of care. This is true—we are doing work that is better than the standard. This dirty trick saves the insurance company from paying the bill.

Every state requires its boards to examine every complaint, and they employ traditionally trained experts. These doctors do not have our background, and they almost universally disapprove of what we do. Some hormone doctors have lost their medical licenses because of a "peer review" like this.

This patient's life was changed by hormone replacement.

Healthcare is freakishly expensive. A month's HGH can be more than a thousand dollars. The rest of the hormones might cost $50 to $100 a month for women.

But you do not have to be rich to get good care. Recall that injectable testosterone used alone is affordable and often adequate. Since it converts into estrogen in the body, patients receive this as well. For women, this is $1 to $2 a week, and for men, about $10 a week.

The following have the potential to make hormone therapy less expensive:

✪ A 10 cc testosterone bottle might last a woman 100 weeks if she used 1/10 cc per week. Compounders are required to put six-month expiration dates on their medications even though they have a much longer shelf life. Also, withdrawing the drug from the bottle so many times can contaminate it. Compounded preparations do not have preservatives, and this increases the risk. (Generic testosterone has preservatives and longer dates.)

✪ Some people buy testosterone made by "underground labs" from bodybuilders at gyms. This costs about the same as at a pharmacy, but there is no doctor fee. I suspect the quality is mostly OK. Syringes are over-the-counter.

I do not recommend any of this, and these practices are against the rules. I consult with doctors about my personal hormone care even though I wrote this book. My physicians are not perfect, but they offer a lot.

The more you understand, the easier it is to find a doctor who is both knowledgeable and reasonably priced. But remember, we all have to make a living.

A GUIDE TO YOUR CLINIC VISIT

Since Trump's executive order in mid-2020, providers may perform consultations virtually, even on the first visit. If patients do not have access to a computer or a smartphone, phone calls are permitted. Prior to this, state medical boards censured physicians for treating people they did not see in person. Hopefully, the new standard will continue under the Democrats.

Here is how hormone clinics work: On your appointment, the physician listens to your story and examines you. Lab tests are drawn, you have a physical exam, and you fill out a general health questionnaire. The doctor answers questions and gives you educational material. Symptom tests such as the following are used.

FOR WOMEN:

Menopause Rating Scale (MRS)

Which of the following symptoms apply to you at this time?

(X ONE Box For EACH Symptom) For Symptoms That Do Not Apply, Please Mark "None").

Symptoms:	none	mild	moderate	severe	extremely severe
Score =	0	1	2	3	4
1. Hot flashes, sweating (episodes of sweating)	☐	☐	☐	☐	☐
2. Heart discomfort (unusual awareness of heart beat, heart skipping, heart racing, tightness)	☐	☐	☐	☐	☐
3. Sleep problems (difficulty in falling asleep, difficulty in sleeping through the night, waking up early)	☐	☐	☐	☐	☐
4. Depressive mood (feeling down, sad, on the verge of tears, lack of drive, mood swings)	☐	☐	☐	☐	☐
5. Irritability (feeling nervous, inner tension, feeling aggressive)	☐	☐	☐	☐	☐
6. Anxiety (inner restlessness, feeling panicky)	☐	☐	☐	☐	☐
7. Physical and mental exhaustion (general decrease in performance, impaired memory, decrease in concentration, forgetfulness)	☐	☐	☐	☐	☐
8. Sexual problems (change in sexual desire, in sexual activity and satisfaction)	☐	☐	☐	☐	☐
9. Bladder problems (difficulty in urinating, increased need to urinate, bladder incontinence)	☐	☐	☐	☐	☐
10. Dryness of vagina (sensation of dryness or burning in the vagina, difficulty with sexual intercourse)	☐	☐	☐	☐	☐
11. Joint and muscular discomfort (pain in the joints, rheumatoid complaints)	☐	☐	☐	☐	☐

FOR MEN:

Which of the following symptoms apply to you at this time? Please, mark the appropriate box for each symptom. For symptoms that do not apply, please mark "none".

Symptoms:	none	mild	moderate	severe	extremely severe
Score =	1	2	3	4	5
1. Decline in your feeling of general well-being (general state of health, subjective feeling)	☐	☐	☐	☐	☐
2. Joint pain and muscular ache (lower back pain, joint pain, pain in a limb, general back ache)	☐	☐	☐	☐	☐
3. Excessive sweating (unexpected/sudden episodes of sweating, hot flushes independent of strain)	☐	☐	☐	☐	☐
4. Sleep problems (difficulty in falling asleep, difficulty in sleeping through, waking up early and feeling tired, poor sleep, sleeplessness)	☐	☐	☐	☐	☐
5. Increased need for sleep, often feeling tired	☐	☐	☐	☐	☐
6. Irritability (feeling aggressive, easily upset about little things, moody)	☐	☐	☐	☐	☐
7. Nervousness (inner tension, restlessness, feeling fidgety)	☐	☐	☐	☐	☐
8. Anxiety (feeling panicky)	☐	☐	☐	☐	☐
9. Physical exhaustion / lacking vitality (general decrease in performance, reduced activity, lacking interest in leisure activities, feeling of getting less done, of achieving less, of having to force oneself to undertake activities)	☐	☐	☐	☐	☐
10. Decrease in muscular strength (feeling of weakness)	☐	☐	☐	☐	☐
11. Depressive mood (feeling down, sad, on the verge of tears, lack of drive, mood swings, feeling nothing is of any use)	☐	☐	☐	☐	☐
12. Feeling that you have passed your peak	☐	☐	☐	☐	☐
13. Feeling burnt out, having hit rock-bottom	☐	☐	☐	☐	☐
14. Decrease in beard growth	☐	☐	☐	☐	☐
15. Decrease in ability/frequency to perform sexually	☐	☐	☐	☐	☐
16. Decrease in the number of morning erections	☐	☐	☐	☐	☐
17. Decrease in sexual desire/libido (lacking pleasure in sex, lacking desire for sexual intercourse)	☐	☐	☐	☐	☐

Have you got any other major symptoms? Yes ☐ No ☐

If Yes, please describe: _____

THANK YOU VERY MUCH FOR YOUR COOPERATION

How questionnaires improve patient care.

The American College and Gynecologists and the Mayo Clinic say that no tests are necessary before replacing hormones for post-menopausal women. So the doctor may or may not wait for laboratory tests to come back before commencing treatment. Follow-up should be every month or two at first. Although you will probably feel far better immediately after starting therapy, these visits are valuable to help you understand the process and fine-tune your therapy. Skipping them is a mistake.

Patients over 50 have many deficiencies. Pills, creams, pellets, injections, and sometimes patches may be used to replace them, and the doses and types of medications should be individualized. The goal is to make each patient look good, feel great, and have improved health. Getting the hormone blood levels optimized does this best.

Hormone adjustment requires patient feedback, and if something is not working, alternatives are usually available. Once the medications are working properly, patients only need to check in once a year for blood work, an interview, and possibly a visit.

PART VII
BONUS CHAPTERS

CHAPTER 25
THE PROSTATE CANCER MEAT GRINDER

Every great cause begins as a movement, becomes a business, and eventually degenerates into a racket.

— ERIC HOFFER

Urology's approach to this disease has undergone an embarrassing outing. The specialty traditionally recommends that the surgeon draw blood for prostate-specific antigen (PSA). The urologists also insert their finger into the patient's rectum to feel for prostate lumps.

If the blood test is high, or the surgeon feels nodules, they stick a large needle repeatedly through the rectum into the prostate to get tissue samples. If the biopsy shows cancer, urologists recommend perilous surgeries or other alarming therapies. This system has been discredited because it never improved survival rates for early disease.

The cancer is present but inactive in most men over 50. Only about twelve percent of men will be diagnosed with prostate cancer during their lives, and their five-year relative survival rate for this cancer after it is diagnosed (the percent with the disease who are alive compared to matched controls) is 97.8 percent. Ignoring it in the early stages produces the same results as treatment, but without the horrific surgical complications. The commonly performed operation, a radical prostatectomy, causes death in 1/200. Compromised or ruined sexuality and uncontrollable urination requiring diapers are common, often for the rest of a man's life.

Some patients already have metastatic cancer before surgery. In these cases, it kills the patient even though he has suffered through the grisly procedure and recovery.

The PSA test is unreliable. It increases with any irritation of the gland due to factors such as infection or even bicycle riding. Antibiotics or anti-inflammatories are the treatments, not surgery. The vast majority of these tumors grow so slowly that death occurs from something else before the disease becomes an issue. PSA is little help to identify aggressive cancers that would be fatal.

Here is a little math: The USPSTF (US Preventive Services Task Force) did a large-scale analysis of the research literature. They concluded that for every 1,000 men ages 55 to 69 who had their PSA checked every one to four years for a decade, it would save one man from prostate cancer. The number needed to test is 1000, over 10,000 patient-years, and who knows how many tests, possibly 50,000.

Even if you believe these small numbers are meaningful, the cost-benefit ratio is terrible. False-positive PSAs lead to biopsies, which have complications just like the true positives. Men with biopsies that show cancer get surgery or other treatments. The harms resulting from these interventions include erectile dysfunction, urinary incontinence, serious cardiovascular events, deep vein thrombosis, pulmonary embolism, and occasionally death. Checking PSA in asymptomatic men produces no improvement in survival.

The American Veterans Administration "PIVOT" trial compared surgery versus observation for localized prostate cancer over 13 years. There was no statistically or clinically significant difference in either all-cause (absolute survival) or even disease-specific mortality (relative survival). Prostate removal surgery is a net harm.

A Scandinavian study looked at 695 men with prostate cancer. They were divided into two groups. One had radical prostatectomy surgery, the other "watchful waiting." With the surgery, the men were half as likely to die of the cancer (relative death rate). Their overall death rates from all causes (absolute deaths) at five and ten years were identical to those who did not have the surgery. Other researchers support these results.

By 2013, urologists partially responded to the heckling from the rest of the medical community. Their new guidelines recommended "individualizing" this test using "shared decision making" between physicians and patients for ages 55 to 69. This is misguided. Otis Brawley, head of the American Cancer Society until 2018, told the story of an unfortunate patient who was victimized by this system in his book *How We Do Harm* (2012):

Ralph entered the prostate cancer meat-grinder after he had his PSA drawn in a shopping mall at a free cancer screening event. It was 4.3. He had twelve painful biopsies. Two of them showed a moderate grade cancer in about fifteen (15) percent of each specimen. Ralph read everything he could. He decided on robotic surgery because the advertising said it was "advanced." It left him impotent and incontinent, and he required diapers for the rest of his life. His PSA several months later was .9. It would have been zero if the surgeon had entirely removed his prostate. He became obsessed with the idea that he still had cancer. So he went to a radiation oncologist who obligingly treated him with "proton beam therapy." When he began seeing blood in his stools later, his surgeons found a fistula. This is a connection between his urethra (urine tube) and his bowel. It was confirmed when he began passing bowel gas from his penis. The surgeons treated him by sewing his colon to the front of his abdomen with a "colostomy," which required him to change a bag containing his stool several times a day. They also created a similar passage from his bladder to his belly, a urostomy. He still had both when he died of a severe urinary infection a few years later. He was 72.

The urologists, or at least the male ones, do not seem to understand the PSA math. Eighty percent of them, along with half the internal medicine specialists, continue to test their own PSAs. Patients have little chance of understanding any of this if most physicians do not.

Like other diseases with expensive treatments, the prostate cancer industry has nonprofit "advocacy" associations growing in a dense thicket all around it. These universally promote PSA screening, which starts the cascade of billions of dollars of medical services. One organization, *Us TOO*, is 90 percent funded by the pharmaceutical and device companies that profit from this prostate circus. *Zero*, formerly the National Prostate Cancer Coalition, has funding from Amgen, AstraZeneca, Aventis, Cytogen, Merck, Pharmacia, and Pfizer.

Kimberly-Clark, the maker of Depends incontinence diapers, is another donor. Prostate cancer surgery sells a *lot* of adult diapers for them, and in 2021, they are advertising on TV using images of rough-looking senior men in diapers. Zero and the others claim to be independent, unbiased grassroots groups that are not beholden to any company.

Shared decision-making is an abdication of responsibility. We are losing trust in advisers who cannot advise. Fewer and fewer will shoulder responsibility in this age of lawsuits. *Other People's Money*, a book about finance, explains the issue: "A good lawyer manages our problem; a bad lawyer responds to every issue by asking us what we want to do. When ill, we look for a recommended course of action, not a detailed description of our ailments and a list of references to relevant medical texts. The demand for transparency in finance is a symptom of the breakdown of trust."

I recommend men pretend they do not have a prostate unless they get symptoms. (*Disclaimer*: I am not a prostate specialist. There may be advantages to these treatments that I did not find. Prostate cancer therapy has common themes with the rest of medicine, however. It is complex and there are conflicts of interest. The treatment studies have large numbers, small differences, and outsize claims.)

Many men cannot wrap their heads around the idea that they should not allow urologists to mess with their prostate. If you still do not get it and you think that there is merit in identifying prostate cancer at an early stage, consider magnetic resonance imaging (MRI) and, if necessary, laser treatment by a radiologist. These are currently the least invasive test and therapy. If the MRI shows a tumor is likely, an imaging specialist can put a guided sampling needle into the suspicious area(s). This results in a diagnosis rate of 90 percent after only one or two sticks.

Contrast this with the usual dozen "random" biopsies that discover only about half of the cancers. You are left sore and in limbo, anticipating a new round of biopsies a year later. Or, if you received a cancer diagnosis, you have to start considering radiation or horrifying, ineffective surgery on your most private parts.

With MRI guidance, however, a laser can be used accurately to burn tiny spots of cancer. You do not get complications from surgery or radiation you never have. Only a few centers in the USA offer this expensive but safe and accurate method. These include Desert Medical Imaging (now Halo Diagnostics) in Palm Springs, CA, and with affiliates nationwide. They also offer a non-invasive treatment for benign prostatic hypertrophy using this same technology.

Since radical prostatectomy for prostate cancer is a multi-billion-dollar surgical industry, these radiologists receive a brutal reception at urological surgery meetings and are not allowed to speak. But the standard approaches are outdated, deforming, require years of care, and the math does not support them.

Note well: all of these therapies are doubtful because the radiologists, like the surgeons, mostly treat low-grade prostate cancer, which rarely kills anyone. Since I can do without needles stuck in my tender places, I refuse to check my PSA ever again unless I have *symptoms*.

Prostate cancer that has spread or metastasized outside the gland is a different issue. This has been treated effectively and inexpensively using synthetic estrogen for more than 50 years. Some doctors still do this. Bio-identical estradiol is available now and should be used instead of the older estrogen compounds. For many patients, this suppresses the tumor, and they feel fine. The PSA should be checked at intervals to be sure.

Casodex and Lupron are the patented, expensive anti-testosterone drugs that are the current "standard of care" for metastatic prostate cancer treatment. They typically work for about five years, then cancer comes back. They cause heart disease, Alzheimer's, osteoporosis, and make patients feel terrible. Otis Brawley speculates that they produce more deaths than they prevent.

This chapter was excerpted from *Butchered by "Healthcare."*

CHAPTER 26
THE FDA PROTECTS THE BIG DRUG COMPANIES

We don't have safe drugs. The drug industry more or less controls itself; our politicians have weakened the regulatory demands over the years, as they think more about money than patient safety; there are conflicts of interest at drug agencies; the system builds on trust, although we know the industry lies to us; and when problems arise, the agencies use fake fixes although they know they won't work... If the American people knew some of the things that went on at the FDA, they'd never take anything but Bayer aspirin.

— LEN LUTWALK, FDA SCIENTIST

In recent decades, FDA oversight has broken down. An editorial in the *BMJ* (2015), "The FDA's New Clothes," said the vast majority of the drugs approved by the FDA from 1978 to 1989 were ineffective. One in five causes serious harm after approval. A second analysis by the same authors reports that 80 to 90 percent of the newest drugs were not improvements over older ones.

FDA whistleblowers have reported what was happening.

Ronald Kavanagh, Ph.D., is a pharmacist who reviewed medications for the FDA from 1998 to 2008. Martha Rosenberg interviewed him:

> [The] honest employee fears the dishonest employee. There is also irrefutable evidence that managers at CDER (Center for Drug Evaluation and Research of the FDA) have placed the nation at risk by corrupting the evaluation of drugs and by interfering with our ability to ensure the safety and efficacy of drugs. While I was at FDA, drug reviewers were clearly told not to question drug companies and that our job was to approve drugs. We were prevented, except in rare instances, from presenting findings at advisory committees. In 2007, formal policies were instituted so that speaking in any way that could reflect poorly on the agency could result in termination. If we asked questions that could delay or prevent a drug's approval - which of course was our job as drug reviewers - management would reprimand us, reassign us, hold secret meetings about us, and worse. Obviously, in such an environment, people will self-censor...I frequently found companies submitting certain data to one place and other data to another place and safety information elsewhere so it could not all be pulled together and then coming in for a meeting to obtain an agreement and proposing that the safety issue is negligible and does not need further evaluation... Sometimes we were literally instructed to only read a 100-150 page summary and to accept drug company claims without examining the actual data, which on multiple occasions I found directly contradicted the summary document. Other times I was ordered not to review certain sections of the submission, but invariably that's where the safety issues would be. This could only occur if FDA management was told about issues in the submission before it had even been reviewed. In addition, management would overload us with huge amounts of material that could not possibly be read by a given deadline and would withhold assistance. When you are able to dig in, if you found issues that would make you turn down a drug, you could be pressured to reverse

*your decision or the review would then be handed off to someone who
would simply copy and paste whatever claims the company made in
the summary document... One manager threatened my children - who
had just turned 4 and 7 years old - and in one large staff meeting, I
was referred to as a "saboteur." Based on other things that happened
and were said, I was afraid that I could be killed for talking to
Congress and criminal investigators... I found evidence of insider
trading of drug company stocks reflecting knowledge that likely only
FDA management would have known. I believe I also have
documentation of falsification of documents, fraud, perjury, and
widespread racketeering, including witness tampering and witness
retaliation.*

Of the 5,918 FDA scientists who responded to a 2006 survey
by the Union of Concerned Scientists, a fifth said their superiors
asked them to exclude, alter, or falsely interpret their conclusions. They were often pressured to approve drugs despite
safety concerns. A follow-up survey in 2011 found they feared
retribution if they wrote about this in journals or spoke to the
press. Many said that political and business interests affect the
FDA's decisions. Over a third felt that a superior had interfered
with their work in the past year. The Institute of Medicine
reported the same year that there was significant outside inter-
ference with the FDA's scientific work.

Early history: The FDA's mission is to protect health by evaluating and approving food, drugs, vaccines, tobacco, supplements, cosmetics, blood transfusions, medical devices, and
veterinary products. The agency oversees 20 percent of the US
economy. The pharmaceutical companies are required to
perform drug studies according to an elaborate set of rules and
present them to the FDA.

The FDA made its reputation in the 1950s when it saved
Americans from congenital disabilities caused by thalidomide. A
German pharmaceutical company marketed this drug almost

without prior study. Its use was for sleep, anxiety, and morning sickness of pregnancy. It was sold over-the-counter in West Germany and other countries.

In the rest of the world, at least ten thousand babies born from mothers who had taken the drug had missing limbs, eyes, and ears. Half the babies died. Many adults who took the drug had nerve damage.

A heroine FDA regulator had her doubts and stalled its approval. Thanks to her, the thalidomide tragedy here did not reach the scale that it did in Europe. But the company passed out unapproved thalidomide samples and performed two trials on 20,000 patients, resulting in patient harm. As a result, in 1962 the US passed laws that directed manufacturers to prove to the FDA their products worked and were safe before they market them. Prescriptions were required for new drugs.

> *The FDA, by spinelessly knuckling under to every whim of the drug companies, has thrown away its high reputation, and in so doing, forfeited our trust.*
>
> — *DRUMMOND RENNIE, DEPUTY EDITOR OF JAMA*

In recent years, however, direct payments from drugmakers to the FDA took the oversight process hostage. Since 2002, pharmaceutical companies have paid about two-thirds of the FDA's $4.7 billion budget through "user fees." This money from the industry goes straight to the FDA, mostly during the patent process. Critics have said the companies should pay taxes instead. In 2007, four retired FDA commissioners agreed: the system creates the wrong incentives. Jessica Wapner, in a PLOS blog, wrote that the structure puts the FDA in the pockets of the drug industry.

Any student of influence understands how and why this

works. The payments, totaling over $3 billion in 2016 alone, create enormous leverage. Michael A. Carome, Director, Public Citizen's Health Research Group, concluded, "User fees fundamentally changed the relationship between the FDA and the pharmaceutical industry such that the agency now views the industry as a partner and a client, rather than a regulated entity." Megan McArdle coined a name for this in a *Bloomberg* article: *regulatory capture.* She says that the regulators who are in place "to tame the wild beasts of business instead become tools of the corporations they regulate."

Congress ignored naysayers and ratified the US arrangement again in 2017. The UK has similar issues. There, drug companies pay 70 percent of the budget of their corresponding regulatory agency, the National Institute for Health and Care Excellence (NICE). Worse: sizable and open payoffs occur *after* the approval process. These reward cooperative FDA advisors on the committees responsible for endorsing drugs.

In 2006, the FDA made it harder for a consumer to sue a pharmaceutical company for harm. The corporations had been trying for decades to get such a law passed through the legislature. It finally influenced someone at the FDA to sneak the measure through as a simple regulation. This created immunity for manufacturers unless plaintiffs proved that a company intentionally committed fraud, which is a high legal barrier.

FDA safety officer David Graham said in a 2004 congressional hearing, "I would argue that the FDA, as currently configured, is incapable of protecting America against another Vioxx [a drug removed from the market for causing fatalities]… Simply put, the FDA and its Center for Drug Evaluation and Research are broken."

How it all started: In 1992, the FDA began a sped-up drug approval process. This was an incentive to get medicines to the market sooner in response to the HIV epidemic. They allowed "surrogate" outcomes such as lab tests rather than requiring "hard" clinical outcomes such as death or heart attack. And they mandated only a single study. The FDA approved the HIV drugs based on increases in the T white blood cell counts and decreases in blood virus counts. Post-marketing surveillance was to have accompanied the scheme, but the Agency never correctly implemented it.

After the start of the accelerated approval process, a review a few years later found that a full third of the drugs approved by the FDA had safety issues. But there were few recalls. They ultimately only took one medication in twenty off the market. If there was regulatory action, it usually consisted solely of a "black-box" warning on the drug label about the possibility of serious harm. The drugmakers bitterly opposed this step because it limits profiteering. For example, Singulair, a pricey asthma medication, causes psychiatric disasters including suicide, but so far there is no black box because of industry resistance.

The FDA permits data scams. Researchers from the Yale University School of Medicine looked at trials between 2005 and 2012. They found that the FDA based many drug approvals on studies that used various forms of data cheating. Donald Light and Ben Goldacre separately confirmed this story. They wrote:

✪ Thirty-seven percent of the drugs had only a single study.

✪ Forty-five percent of the trials for drug approval used study endpoints such as blood sugar or cholesterol (surrogate markers) rather than hard endpoints such as death or another clinical finding.

✪ Nearly a third of all the studies made a comparison with an older drug. When two drugs are found to be about the same, the companies usually claim some obscure advantage for the recent one. This games the approval process and allows the corporations to market expensive "me-too" medications that offer no benefit over the older ones.

✪ To make a drug look good, the companies often exclude

people who are more likely to have adverse outcomes. Other times, they use people who are more likely to have side effects, which can make an older drug look bad.

✪ When companies do nonrandomized trials on unrepresentative populations, they can create almost any result.

✪ Experiments are sometimes run that lack a comparator or control arm. This is called a single-arm trial and has little validity.

✪ Some experimenters do approval studies that are not randomized, controlled, and double-blinded, which is the current standard of proof. Some allow studies that are easily unblinded.

✪ To show benefit, sometimes doses of a test drug are used that are too high for routine clinical use. These studies last long enough to show benefits but are kept short enough to conceal adverse reactions.

✪ The other way this is played is to use high doses of the comparison drug. This creates side effects that make the new drug look great by comparison.

✪ Another often-used ploy is inaccurate measurement and improper reporting of the number needed to treat and the number needed to harm.

✪ Huge trials are sometimes stopped early because results appear beneficial or harmful at that point. This prevents full evaluation and complete reporting.

Physicians should be trained to detect these commonplace forms of deceit when reading medical journals. I spotted them as I learned more.

IN A 2012 BMJ EDITORIAL ANALYSIS, DONALD LIGHT AND JOEL Lexchin wrote that, of all the new products developed in the past 50 years, 85-90 percent produced many harms but few benefits. Most of them are me-too drugs used for established markets. They are not improvements. These medications are 80 percent of the US's increase in drug spending.

Despite the sad deterioration of the FDA, it is still the most respected and active organization of its kind in the world. Many of its people are idealistic and well-meaning, and they try to maintain standards. They are the only barrier between US consumers and pharmaceutical disasters. To their credit, the FDA is mostly successful at keeping shoddy drugs out of the US. Foreign manufacturers sell these with impunity in Brazil, Africa, Mexico, and Eastern Europe.

POSTSCRIPT: Since a 1975 law was passed, expiration dates were required for drugs. A pharmacist who recalls this event says that his knowledgeable colleagues thought it was ridiculous. But they quickly realized it boosted sales.

In a 2006 study of 122 expired drugs, two-thirds of them were stable in every tested lot. Their sell-by dates were over four years too early. The US military, the CDC, and the Department of Defense understand this and for decades have saved billions of dollars by stockpiling outdated drugs. But the Pharmaceutical Research and Manufacturers of America (PhRMA) lobby claims the short expiration dates are all about safety.

This chapter was excerpted from *Butchered by "Healthcare."*

CHAPTER 27

THE JOURNALS' SINS ARE THE
EDITORS' SINS

*If you don't read the newspaper, you're uninformed. If you read the
newspaper, you're misinformed.*

— MARK TWAIN

Corporate funding has made medical journals wealthy.
When I trained 35 years ago, they were everywhere, but
with the cash injection you will read about below, they have
become a blizzard of paper on every surface of a doctor's house
and office. To scan the primary care articles alone would take
hundreds of hours a month. Over 5,000 journal articles get
published every day.

Physicians get their information from journals, and the
editors are responsible for everything that gets printed. They are
the most sophisticated people in healthcare, and they understand what is happening as it occurs. But they only speak up
after they retire because they do not want to lose their presti-
gious, lucrative jobs (I am guilty of this, too).

The following are two of their confessionals. There are similar statements published about *NEJM, JAMA,* and others.

> *Journals have devolved into information laundering operations for the pharmaceutical industry.* The case against science is straightforward: much of the scientific literature, perhaps half, may simply be untrue. Afflicted by studies with small sample sizes, tiny effects, invalid exploratory analyses, and flagrant conflicts of interest, together with an obsession for pursuing fashionable trends of dubious importance, science has taken a turn towards darkness.
>
> — RICHARD HORTON, *LANCET* EDITOR
>
> *Medical journals are an extension of the marketing arm of pharmaceutical companies....* between two-thirds and three-quarters of the trials published in the major journals—Annals of Internal Medicine, JAMA, Lancet, and New England Journal of Medicine—are funded by the industry.
>
> — RICHARD SMITH, EDITOR, *BRITISH MEDICAL JOURNAL* AND AUTHOR, *THE TROUBLE WITH MEDICAL JOURNALS* (2006)

About half of journal revenue comes directly from drug companies. Perhaps 90 percent of the articles and research are industry-funded, and the corporate contractors ghostwrite the majority. Marcia Angell, the *NEJM* editor for 20 years, told how they do it in *The Truth About the Drug Companies* (2004), "I saw companies begin to exercise a level of control over the way research is done that was unheard of when I first came to the journal... It is simply no longer possible to believe much of the clinical research that is published, or to rely on the judgment of trusted physicians or authoritative medical guidelines."

A review of 370 drug studies in 2003 showed that company-sponsored trials were much more likely to have positive results than when funding was from other sources. A single positive trial may be printed and reprinted in hundreds of different venues and forms. The core of science is unfavorable reports, but these are frequently concealed. For example, during the approval process for the influenza treatment Tamiflu, the drug company withheld Australian studies that suggested the drug was worthless.

If a journal publishes something their industry sponsors dislike, they will threaten them with loss of advertising or worse. *Annals of Internal Medicine* (June 1992) made the mistake of publishing Michael Wilkes' study about drug advertising harms. The NEJM and JAMA had turned down the article.

In punishment, the big corporations withdrew advertising from the *Annals*, and they lost over a million dollars in revenue. Two respected editors lost their jobs. After this, US journals allowed pharmaceutical companies to print written rebuttals of any study they did not like in the same issue as the study. Neither big tobacco nor big food has ever received a concession like this.

Journals make startling amounts of money. Profit margins at scientific publishing companies average a sensational 35 percent. Other successful publishers worldwide average 10 percent, and industries without subsidies are successful at 10 percent. Reed Elsevier, the largest medical publisher, is stunningly profitable:

YEAR:	REVENUE:	NET:	PROFIT:
2016	3.28 B	1.22 B	37%
2010	2.58 B	933 M	36%

How do they do it? Journals' expenses are modest. The companies, federal grants, and academia pay for studies, so these are free. Review editors and members of editorial boards are mostly unpaid volunteers. Revenues are huge, however. A single journal subscription may cost several thousand dollars a year. Reprinted articles from a journal often cost $50 each. Comprehensive literature searches can cost tens of thousands of dollars to get the full texts.

Journals were billing Harvard's library $3.5 million a year for subscriptions. It had to cut some journals from its list because of these ever-increasing costs. In 2019, the University of Southern California ended its subscription to Elsevier's journals because of the exorbitant prices.

Reprints make money for the journals because they sell them right back to the study sponsors. These companies typically pay for the entire charade, from study design to research grants to ghostwriting. Salespeople gift purchased articles to doctors to prove that the drugs work. This is a page from the corporate sales and influence playbook. Dr. Deepak Malhotra described the way it works in the *BMJ*: "As a medical director of a pharmaceutical company, I learnt how to get articles published in journals, with one journal promising publication if we purchased 2000 reprints at $10 each."

The *NEJM's* publisher gets 23% of its income from reprints. *The Lancet*—41%. *JAMA* receives 53%. In a 2012 study, reprint income per article for the *Lancet* was a median of £287,353 ($363,946), with the most profitable one £1,551,794. Industry funding was ten times more likely in the most reprinted articles. Journal volumes labeled "special editions" are advertising vehicles. They look like the others but usually describe only a single therapy, and the journal editors do not expect them to have high scientific standards. One drug company typically supplies nearly the entire budget.

Occasionally, a corporation will fabricate an entire journal, and they look legitimate. Merck created the *Australasian Journal of Bone and Joint Medicine* to advertise Fosamax. Recall the

Disease-Mongering chapter; this drug's utility is doubtful. The Medline database did not index this journal, and it had no website. Elsevier published the magazine for several months, then it vanished.

The industry pays journal editors directly, and they get their salaries in addition. Jeanne Lenzer describes how the device companies use this power:

> *A medical journal editor who received millions of dollars from a medical device manufacturer wrote and edited articles favourable to the manufacturer without stating his conflict of interests to readers. Thomas Zdeblick, a University of Wisconsin orthopaedic surgeon… editor-in-chief of the Journal of Spinal Disorders & Techniques in 2002, received more than $20m… in patent royalties, and $2m in consulting fees from Medtronic for spinal implants sold by the company during his tenure as editor.*
>
> — *BMJ* (2010)

Jason Fung, a Canadian academic nephrologist, summarizes these payouts in a blog:

> *Of all journal editors that could be assessed, 50.6% were on the take. The average payment in 2014 was $27,564. Each. This does not include an average $37,330 given for 'research' payments… Each editor of the Journal of the American College of Cardiology received, on average, $475,072 personally and another $119,407 for research. With 35 editors, that's about $15 million in money for editors. No wonder the JACC loves drugs and devices.*
>
> — MEDIUM.COM (2018)

The massive advertising revenues, the reprint deals, and the payoffs to the editors create near-complete corporate control of the only physician information source. We support the drug-makers and device manufacturers with insurance and govern-ment dollars, and they pay the journals and editors. The "big five" most respected medical journals, Lancet, JAMA, BMJ, NEJM, and Annals of Internal Medicine, are all contaminated with this commercial bias. The BMJ has the most integrity, at least by one measure. Only three percent of its revenues come from reprints.

Business corrupts science when it pays for research. Nortin Hadler wrote in *The Citizen Patient* (2013): "It turns out that the vast majority of the clinical literature is so lacking in method-ological quality as to offer no contribution of substance to clin-ical decision making. For most clinical questions, one is fortunate to find a dozen studies that can be deemed informa-tive." Gøtzsche is franker: "The pervasive scientific misconduct has led to a research literature where one has to dig deeply to find the few gems among all the garbage."

This chapter was excerpted from *Butchered by "Healthcare."*

APPENDIX A: THYROID DOSING IS AN ART

If you have thyroid disease or treat it, this appendix is vital.

> Alice: *Wow, it is unreal to find so many people with common symptoms. I also have tried all the synthetic drugs out there, even a mixture of them for the past eight years. I had every symptom that a lack of thyroid can cause. I have gained so much weight and stay swollen. Last month I requested Armour from my doctor, and I'm feeling much better. I lost eleven pounds. I am in a better frame of mind and have more energy. I really do not understand why a doctor who sees that the synthetic brands are not helping does not switch you to a natural thyroid... We have no control.*

Robert Morgan is a hypothyroidism expert. He says:
My goal is—first and always—to make my patients feel good. To do this, I try to bring both T4 and T3 into the upper-normal range. So I check them both. If the T4 is low, I often start by with that. This may be all they need if the T4 to T3 conversion process is working. But if the first laboratory test shows a low T3, I prescribe porcine thyroid.

*I base my starting dose on weight, as recommended by the manu-
facturer. For T4, the full dose is 1.6 mcg per kg per day. A 160-pound
woman weighs 73 kg. This is roughly a dose of 117 mcg or .117 mg.
(T4 is supplied in many doses, including .112 and .125 mg.) If patients
are elderly or have medical problems, I may begin lower. The key is
careful follow-up and communication with the patient. I worry about
them first and the labs second. Depending on what happens to the
symptoms and numbers, I sometimes prescribe Cytomel (pure T3) as
well.*

*Your doctor should learn what tests their lab does best. Total T3
and T4 hormone levels are fine, but "free" T3 and T4 might be considered as well. These are more active because they are not "bound" to
blood proteins. TSH confuses everyone, its results are inconsistent, and
it is useless for treatment evaluation. Its only place is as a test to screen
people suspected of thyroid disease.*

*Psychiatrists prescribe large doses of T4 because they never
learned to treat both T3 and T4. Their goal should be to get each of
these tests into the high-normal range using combinations of T4,
porcine, and Cytomel (T3). This requires patience. If they learned how
to do this, their depression patients would need less total medication.
Treating depression with thyroid is successful, and every primary care
doctor should try it before considering Prozac or other
antidepressants.*

Vulnerable, fragile patients should be started on half of the
standard thyroid dose. These include elderly patients, those
with heart disease, and people with longstanding hypothyroidism. They must be coached to continue the drug as we
increase the dose, even if they do not start to feel better immediately. If they are not followed carefully, some lose patience with
the new medications and quit them. So we try to prescribe an
accurate dose at the start.

Porcine helps patients understand they are improving
because T3 reaches a high blood level within three hours (it is
gone in a couple of days). That is why dosing porcine twice a

day helps relieve late afternoon fatigue. T3 can interfere with sleep if taken at night, so we do not give it past noon.

If the patient needs T4, the generics are less reliable than Synthroid, so many of us stopped prescribing them. T4 lasts over a week in the body. If used alone, several weeks go by before patients usually appreciate a dose change. Split dosing does not improve responses, and some patients take it in the evening and have no trouble sleeping.

For best relief of fatigue and other symptoms, months of careful thyroid adjustment may be required. When people get too much, jitteriness and nervousness develop. This is usually obvious. The most common mistake, however, is under-dosing. T3 and T4 (and/or the free versions) should be rechecked a month or two after starting therapy. (Author's note: Recent studies published in the BMJ say that raising T3 improves symptoms more than raising T4.)

The proper dose of porcine ranges from 1.5 grains a day to two grains (130 mg) twice a day or more. When T4 is used by itself, patients need between .075 and .175 mg daily, rarely exceeding .2 mg (this is the same as 75 to 175 micrograms, rarely exceeding 200 mcg). For best absorption, all thyroids should be taken on an empty stomach, at least a half-hour before eating or even drinking coffee.

If pork thyroid was over-the-counter in the USA as it is in Thailand, tens of thousands of people could see for themselves if they responded. Perhaps our addiction to antidepressants would decrease. A few would get toxicity, but when this happened, most would simply quit the drugs. Note: Some US patients buy thyroid on Thai websites. The potency can be low, but it costs a tenth of the same thing in the US per grain.

LEVOTHYROXINE TO PORCINE CONVERSION: Charts such as this only help at the beginning of therapy. After this, doses should be adjusted based on the response, side effects, and lab numbers.

LEVOTHYROXINE: (T4 ONLY)
100 mcg=.1 mg *low standard dose*
150 mcg=.15 mg *standard dose*
<u>200 mcg=.2 mg *high standard dose*</u>
PORCINE THYROID IN GRAINS:
1 GRAIN IS 65 MG OF DRIED PORK,
CONTAINS BOTH T3 AND T4. T3 IS
<u>**ABOUT 4X MORE POTENT THAN T4**</u>
1 grain=65 mg pill, has 38 mcg (.038 mg)
T4 and 9 mcg (.009 mg) of T3
2 grains=130 mg pill, has 76 mcg (.076 mg)
of T4 plus 18 mcg (.018 mg) of T3
76 + 4 x 18 = 148 mcg = .148 mg "equivalent"
To T4.   *Standard dose*
2.5 grains=162 mg pill has 95 mcg (.095 mg)
Of T4 plus 23 mcg (.023 mg) of T3
= 187 mcg = .187 mg "equivalent" to T4
Higher standard dose
3 grains=195 mg pill has 114 mcg (.114 mg)
Of T4 plus 27 mcg (.027 mg) of T3
= 222 mcg or about .2 mg "equivalent" to T4
<u>*A still higher dose*</u>

APPENDIX B: BLOOD TESTING AND DOSING REVIEW

Doctors should treat *you* rather than your tests. The laboratory is useful but overrated—how you feel is the key thing. Levels are guidelines and not absolute rules. The doctor checks the tests at the start of therapy. Later, the numbers reveal whether you are getting enough hormone—or sometimes, if you are getting any. Occasional patients are found to be overdoing it.

Patient feedback helps. For example, I had a 61-year-old who said she felt energized, alert, and thinks clearly while using the estrogen patch. But when she took only the compounded estradiol capsules, she did not do as well. She then discovered a brand name estradiol pill from a foreign country that made her feel as good as the patch. It was not available here and was inexpensive there. (Note: for the best health protection, she might try the patch and also take the oral drug as well.) Although the brand-names have excellent quality control, they are not available for every hormone and may not be the right formulation or strength.

From Dana's website: *When my free T3 levels reached the top quarter of the normal range, it was like magic. One by one, my hypothyroidism symptoms disappeared. I felt so good I cried.*

Critical point: blood test numbers vary depending on the time interval between taking the medicine and drawing the blood. Levels are high right after the dose and lower later. For the once-a-day drugs, testing about five to six hours after the medication is taken gives consistent results. Longer-acting medications, such as once a week injectable testosterone, show high blood levels for several days, then decline. Common sense and experience are needed to understand the patient, their symptoms, the proper doses, and their test results.

Most hormone doctors aim for the blood levels seen in young, healthy adults. Abe Morgentaler, the Harvard testosterone expert, recommends levels in the "mid to upper-normal range to optimize the response to treatment." This is protective and safe.

When we are young, our bodies are sensitive and might only need moderate hormone levels. Some men at 20 years old have a testosterone level of 700 ng/dl, which gives them a healthy interest in sex and rapid response to exercise. A man of 65 might be less sensitive and need fifteen hundred ng/dl to feel and perform his best.

Health is closely related to how you feel. But even if you feel fine already, and your levels are low, your health will probably improve with hormone supplementation. You might get the most benefit if you use doses in the upper range and have higher blood levels. For best results, work with your doctor and follow up with blood tests.

The following are approximate desirable blood levels for hormone replacement:

∾

TESTOSTERONE, Men: 1000 to 2000 ng/dl. Best improvement in cholesterol with 1500 to 2000 ng/dl, Estrogen levels rise at this T level. Sexuality may be better at intermediate levels such as 1200-1500. This is individual and must be tried.

TESTOSTERONE, women: 250 to 300 ng/dl. Many authorities check free testosterone, but each lab is different for this test. For simplicity's sake, these numbers are for total blood testosterone.

PROGESTERONE, women: 10 to 20 or even 30 ng/ml (higher if bleeding needs to be suppressed). Sometimes high levels are required to get best symptom relief. Progesterone is harmless.

ESTROGEN, women: 75 to 100 pg/ml. is normal before menopause. Levels are frequently many times higher in young women, depending on the time of the month. Cholesterol and blood count improve if the levels are raised this high. Oral progesterone may decrease estrogen absorption, so when it is taken, the estrogen dose may need to be increased.

ESTROGEN, men: 50 to 70 pg/ml, but not usually measured. Some experts are now recommending estradiol use if levels are low despite testosterone administration (which raises estradiol).

This is a new trend.

Estrogen blockers are toxic and are not for everyday use.

Notes: 1) estrogen is heart protective 2) testosterone gets converted to estrogen 3) do not block estrogen except temporarily for gynecomastia or for cancers

DHEA-s, women: 250 ng/ml, but this is a minimum. For older women, large doses often help, and high levels often work best for joints. Young women: acne and hair growth. Lower doses are often best. No other harmful effects.

DHEA-s, men: 400 to 600 ng/ml

VITAMIN D 60 to 100 ng/ml. Possible toxicity issues with levels over 130. Starting D3 dose: 5000 IU/day if patient is under 200 lb, 10,000 IU/day if over 200 lb. Check levels; adjust as needed.

THYROID Boost the T3/T4 to upper normal levels or symptomatic relief. Free T3 about 4.2 pg/ml is optimal. Some generic T4s are weak, consider switching to Synthroid. Women sense the improvement more than men. TSH should be ignored. If measured, should be less than one (suppressed), and .1 is fine.

MELATONIN blood levels not used

HGH Increase to about .6 mg/day

(two units). Most treat based on
dose, but if blood testing
is desired, the IGF-1 level
(serum-insulin-like-growth-factor-1)
should be 300 to 350 ng/ml.

Lifeextension.com offers hormone blood testing without a prescription for as little as $250. See: "hormone testing for men" or "hormone testing for women." Check out and pay, then print up the lab sheet and take it to the LabCorp blood drawing station nearest to you. The results will be emailed to you.

How necessary is blood testing? Most hormone prescribing could be adequately managed by simply watching symptoms, although medical boards are critical of this. This poses a dilemma when patients cannot afford the labs. The Mayo Clinic and the American College of Gynecology say that no tests are needed before prescribing hormones for menopausal women. Labs are a great help for thyroid, however.

HORMONE DOSING:
TESTOSTERONE, men: *cream*: 100-
200 mg/ml, 1-2 ml twice a day.
Inner thigh or scrotal use.
lipoderm cream is better than gel.
Injectable: use testosterone
cypionate or enanthate 200 mg/ml
in oil. 1 ml a week intramuscularly
is the starting dose. Or, .5 ml 2 x
/ week for more steady blood levels.
Pellet: dose is 20 mg per kilogram.

Use 200 mg pellets.
trocar insertion. See also the
Killing Testosterone chapter.
TESTOSTERONE, women: *cream*:
10-50 mg/ml, 1/2 ml 2 x/wk. May
increase to daily for stronger effects.
Injection: enanthate or cypionate
200 mg/ml, 1/10 to 2/10 cc
subcutaneously a week
Pellet dose: 1 mg per pound, approx.
Use 100 mg pellets, which may
be broken in half as needed.
PROGESTERONE, women:
micronized capsules: 100 to 1200
mg at bedtime, limited by sleepiness.
Troches: same dose, no sleepiness.
Used during daytime
Creams: ineffective
PROGESTERONE, men: Never use.
See Frequently Asked Questions
chapter.
ESTROGEN, men: Not conventionally
given to men. They get it from
testosterone breakdown. A few
hormone doctors are giving 1-2
mg estradiol a day to older men with
lower levels, aiming for a level of
about 70 pg/ml. Sexuality improves.
DHEA-S, women: *capsule*, 10-200
mg. The lower amount for young
women (otherwise acne and hair
growth).
DHEA-S, men: *capsule*, 50-200 mg.
VITAMIN D3: *capsule*, 5000 Int'l

units/d if patient wt. under 200
pounds. 10,000 IU per day
day if weight over 200 lb.
Increase dose as
needed to produce levels of 60
to 100 ng/ml.

THYROID: *pill.* (Thyroid chapter)
Measure T3 and T4. Depending on
results, start with either porcine
or T4. Dose T4 (Branded Synthroid
may be the most consistent quality),
Cytomel, and/or pork until patients
feel good or free T3 is about 4.2
picograms per ml and the T4 is
upper-normal. Decrease for
jitteriness, headache, nervousness,
or rapid heart rate.

MELATONIN: women start at 1 mg,
men at 3 mg. *Slow release (SR) cap.*
Increase dose until sound sleep
or side effects. Maximum: 100 mg.

HGH: *Injectable.* Used 5-7 days a week.
Measured in both international
units (IU) and milligrams (mg).
3 IU equals 1 mg. Start at:
.2 mg per day (.6 units), taken
at night, increase slowly every few
weeks to avoid swelling.
Maximum dose: .4 to .6 mg per day.
(1.2-2 IU).
Athletes sometimes use double this
dose or more. (HGH chapter).

~

NOTES:

Testosterone cream: 100 to 200 mg/cc (I like the lipoderm compounding base) is commonly used for men. One cc twice a day may give high enough blood levels, especially if it is rubbed into the scrotum. If the cream is applied to the inner thighs, two cc twice a day may be required. An alcohol gel is available but can be compounded only up to 100 mg/cc. Lipoderm is better absorbed than the gel, and the gel burns if put on the scrotum.

Injectable testosterone: Either do this yourself by looking in a mirror or have a friend or domestic partner do it. To learn how search for "intramuscular injections" and "intramuscular injection sites." I recommend using the upper outer hip and rotating each week between your hips. Slapping or scratching the injection spot before the shot is given will usually make it painless.

This is what the needles and syringes look like.

In most places, you can purchase these over-the-counter from your pharmacy or order them on the internet. I recommend the one cc BD brand syringe with a screw-on "Luer-lock" needle mount. These give a more exact dose than the three cc type. Do not use the "Luer-taper" slip-on mount because the needle may come off when you inject the thick oil.

When removing testosterone from the bottle, most people use a larger needle such as an 18 gauge. When they inject themselves, they use a smaller one. I suggest a 1 inch 25 gauge for men. The oil goes slowly through a 26 or 27-gauge needle, and a full cc might take up to a minute to go in. I don't like needles inside me this long. If you are a woman and are using only 1/10 to 2/1o cc, thinner needles down to about 27 gauge work fine because injection of this small quantity does not take long.

For injections into fat, you may use your belly or your hips where you can see what you are doing. There is no difference in effectiveness between fat and muscle injections, but putting the male dose of a full cc of testosterone into fat stings and may bruise. Women usually inject into fat with a tiny, short needle.

The tip of a needle may bend when you put it into the bottle. If you use the same one to inject yourself, it can be painful. Always clean your skin and the top of the bottle with alcohol and use the syringes and needles only once. After each injection, hold pressure on the spot for a moment to avoid bruising.

The starting dose for men is one cc a week of testosterone cypionate or enanthate, 200 mg/cc. These are nearly identical. Levels the day after the shot may be 2000 ng/dl, but in a week, before the next injection, they may drop to 600-700. Using a half cc twice a week produces more continuous blood levels. This is likely better for your body.

For women, the dose is about 10-20 mg a week, which is 1/10th to 2/10ths of a cc. Some feel better using 3/10 cc. Hair growth, acne, and enlarged clitorises can happen at higher doses, especially for younger women.

Injectable testosterone is the least expensive hormone, costing about $1-2 a week for women and about $10 a week for men. The cream is more. Patches and Androgel are pricey, and blood levels rarely get high enough for the best effects.

Testosterone undecanoate is injectable testosterone lasting three months that is available in Europe.

Ways to take medicines: A long-standing problem is how to make oral medicines work as well as shots. When drugs are taken by mouth, they go through the intestine and liver system, which inactivates many of them. Micronized medications are spread out over particles, which makes them well absorbed orally. Troches get good levels because the drug dissolves in the mouth, rectum, or vagina and enters the body directly without passing through the intestine and liver. Injections put medications right into the blood or adjacent tissues.

Pill testosterone is sometimes useful for older women. This oral route does not work as well because drugs taken by mouth get inactivated. But this group may get enough to benefit because they need so little. And they may regard the sexual effects of higher doses as side effects. The starting dose is a 25 mg capsule.

Testosterone pellets may be the best "feel good" hormone. Some clinics treat both menopause and andropause (the male menopause) solely with these. Pellets last about three months for women and 4-5 months for men. These are placed under the skin into fat. The ones for women are about the size of a rice grain. Men need ten times the female dose, so the pellets and insertion devices are bigger. For women, the procedure is painless, but for men, it is a bigger hassle and can produce soreness lasting up to a month.

Pellet dosing and insertion: The testosterone pellet dose is 1 mg/pound for women. That would be two 100 mg pellets for a 200-pound woman. To insert these, I use a sterile, three-inch 6-gauge hollow needle and a thick piece of sterile wire to hold the pellet in the fat when I withdraw the needle. The dose for men is 20 mg/kilogram, which could be ten 200 mg pellets for a 100 kg (220 lb) man. These are placed in three rows. Men need a much larger 4-gauge hollow needle to accommodate their larger pellets. Doctors can either spend 75 cents for these at a tattoo website such as painfulpleasures.com or buy fancy ones for $250 from the compounders. The wholesale cost of either the 100 or 200 mg pellets is currently $12-17 from Anazao Pharmacy. Pellets may be inserted into fat anywhere on the body. I prefer going through the inside of the belly button to avoid making a visible scar. I always scrub the skin there with chlorhexidine and use plenty of lidocaine local anesthetic inserted with a 2 inch 25-gauge needle.

At the start of hormone supplementation, pellets assure us that patients use the medicine long enough and in high enough doses for them to find out whether it works for them. But in the long run, coming to the office for a minor surgical procedure several times a year might be too much of a hassle, especially for men.

Rebecca Glaser's hormonebalance.org has helpful articles about pellets and testosterone used as the only hormone therapy.

Progesterone: Creams work poorly. Levels of at least 5 ng/ml are required to suppress the uterine lining and prevent uterine cancer, but higher levels of 10-20 are preferable. Even with oral progesterone capsules and troches, levels are frequently under 10. For the best health and performance, increase the dose until the levels are in the desirable range. Taking it twice a day helps.

Vitamin D: over-the-counter D (D3) comes in 1,000, 2,000, 5,000, or 10,000 international unit (IU) capsules. (Vitamin D2 is available by prescription, but it does not work well.) Start at 5000 IU of D3 a day if you are under 200 pounds and 10,000 IU if over 200. The blood level goal is 60 to 100 ng/ml. This should be measured at most once a month because Vitamin D is stored in fat and this takes time to become saturated with the drug. Some people may need 15,000 IU a day or more to get desirable levels. Some sources recommend magnesium, vitamin K, and zinc supplementation if larger D3 doses are taken. Although side effects are rare, the doctor should remain in contact with her patients. Vitamin D toxicity causes high calcium levels with nausea, vomiting, weakness, and frequent urination. If patients have any symptoms, a calcium level should be checked and the D should be stopped.

Melatonin: The long-acting slow-release (SR) type that lasts six hours or longer works best. Compounders make this for each patient by prescription, but at least one source, nutrascriptives.com, sells it over-the-counter. The Life Extension brand has an excellent reputation, but I have no experience with it. Compounded melatonin comes in strengths of 1, 2, 3, and 5 milligrams and higher. Women start at 1 mg and men at 3 mg. Patients are instructed to increase their dosage until sound sleep or side effects occur. Some people do not tolerate it because they dislike the dreams. A few become agitated and must stop.

For extra credit: How to treat metastatic prostate cancer using estradiol. (Disclaimer: like the rest of this book, find a doctor to help you and take responsibility for this process. I supply this information as a starting point for your research.) First, read the articles that describe treatment with synthetic estrogen. These are several decades old. Use micronized estradiol 2 mg per day to start. Every two weeks, increase this by 2 mg until the patient is taking 8 mg a day. Or, start with two mg and go up by one mg each week. Breast tenderness is the limiting side effect. Most men adjust to this well, but a few cannot tolerate it. Draw PSA and estradiol levels at intervals to monitor the process. Often six to eight mg per day will produce an improvement in the PSA. Some patients are too far gone for a cure, but this therapy helps bone pain even if it does not bring down the PSA much. By three months, the PSA has usually responded. An estradiol level of 100 is sometimes high enough for therapeutic effects, but levels of 500-600 may be necessary. These patients may not be interested in sex but feel great. They lose the fatigue and discouragement they get with hormone blocker treatments.

APPENDIX C: HORMONES AND THE BRAIN

These references describe hormone treatment of brain dysfunction—a limited area. They are examples of the vast science backing general hormone therapy. Many thanks to Neal Rouzier, MD, for his herculean work putting most of this list and many other references together. The best introduction to the following is *Estrogen Matters* (2018) by Avrum Bluming and Carol Tavris.

Physicians have as much trouble interpreting this literature as anyone else. They have spent a lifetime in study, know a lot about the industry-sponsored trials, and have trouble reconciling the contradictions. The medical papers they read are written by academics who purposefully muddle what they say with technical, convoluted language. In their defense, if these authors put their work into plain English, they would never find a publisher.

The easiest way to search online for an abstract is to enter the article's title into your browser. If you are reading the e-book, use the link if I provided one. After you have the URL, Sci-hub.st can get you the full text. (Against the law! For entertainment purposes only!) If you want to buy them from legitimate sources, prepare to spend about $40 each.

ESTROGEN AND BRAIN FUNCTION

✪ Hormone replacement therapy and Alzheimer's disease in older women: A systematic review of literature. *Neuroscience and Behavioral Health* Vol.10(1), pp. 1-8, April 2018. A 2017 review. Two-thirds of the trials examined showed that hormone therapy, particularly estrogens, protected against Alzheimer's. They looked at 898 studies and excluded all but 15 because the science was poor. Even these selected papers confused the bio-identicals with the obsolete drugs.

✪ The Potential for Estrogens in Preventing Alzheimer's Disease and Vascular Dementia. *Therapeutic Advances in Neurological Disorders*. 2009 Jan; 2(1): 31–49. Cited hundreds of basic science and animal studies supporting hormone treatment of brain dysfunction including Alzheimer's disease.

✪ The Effect of Estrogen Replacement Therapy on Alzheimer's Disease and Parkinson's Disease in Postmenopausal Women: A Meta-Analysis. *Frontiers of Neuroscience*. 2020 Mar 10;14:157. A meta-analysis of 21 articles in showed preventive efficacy of estrogen for AD.

✪ The mysterious effect of reproductive hormones on cognitive function: scientific knowledge in search of an application. *J Gend Specific Med* 2000 Oct;3(7):33-7. Showed that estrogen inhibits formation of amyloid protein, the brain substance correlated with AD.

✪ Effects of estrogen use on the risk of Alzheimer's disease. Loret De Mola JR. *Biomedicina*. 2000 Jan;3(1):6-7. Review article: Estrogen reduces the formation of amyloid protein. All prospective studies show a reduction of Alzheimers 30 to 70% when estrogen was used.

✪ Impact of Progestins on Estrogen-Induced Neuroprotection: Synergy by Progesterone and 19-Norprogesterone and Antagonism by Medroxyprogesterone Acetate. *Endocrinology*, Volume 143, Issue 1, 1 January 2002, Pages 205–212. Real progesterone, but not the synthetic type, reduces AD according to a study in Neurology.

✪ The women's health initiative reports: Critical review of the findings. Gambrell RD. *The Female Patient*. 2004;29:25-41. When begun at menopause and continued for over 10 years, estrogen therapy produced an 83% reduction in the chances of getting Alzhermer's.

✪ Hormone replacement therapy and incidence of Alzheimer disease in older women: the Cache County Study. Zandi PP, Carlson MC, Plassman BL, et al. *JAMA*. 2002 Nov 6;288(17):2123-2129. AD in hormone users was half that for those who never took hormones. Those who used hormones for a decade or more had 1/5th the chance of getting Alzheimers. The conclusion: this therapy should begin at menopause and never stop.

✪ Confirmed: Surgical Menopause Linked to Cognitive Decline. *Neurology*. Published online December 11, 2013. Female surgical castration of either one or both ovaries, especially at earlier ages, produces higher AD rates.

✪ Estrogen in the prevention of atherosclerosis. A randomized, double-blind, placebo-controlled trial. *Annals of Internal Medicine*. 2001 Dec 4;135(11):939-53. Estrogen prevented artery wall thickening, a measure of atherosclerotic heart disease.

✪ Significance of oestrogens in male (patho)physiology. Gooren LJ, Toorians AW. *Ann Endocrinol*. 2003 Apr;64(2):126-35. Estrogens help bones, brains, and hearts.

✪ Endogenous Sex Hormones and Cardiovascular Disease in Men. Majon Muller, Yvonne T. van der Schouw, Jos H. H. Thijssen, Diederick E. Grobbee. *The Journal of Clinical Endocrinology & Metabolism*, Volume 88, Issue 11, 1 November

2003, Pages 5076–5086. Men with higher estradiol levels had less cardiovascular disease.

❂ Early Postmenopausal Transdermal 17β-Estradiol Therapy and Amyloid-β Deposition. Kantarci et al. (2016). *Journal of Alzheimer's Disease*, 53, 547-556. Estradi0l decreased amyloid deposition, as measured by PET scanning.

❂ Estrogen: A master regulator of bioenergetic systems in the brain and body. Rettberg, J. Yao, J., & Brinton, R. (2013). Weight loss, better glucose metabolism, and higher metabolic rates occurred for those on hormones.

❂ High plasma estradiol interacts with diabetes on risk of dementia in older postmenopausal women. Carcaillon, L., Brailly-Tabard, S., Ancelin, M.-L., Rouaud, O., Dartigues, J.-F., Cuiochon-Mantel, A., & Scarabin, P.-Y. (2014). *American Academy of Neurology*, 504-511. Although increased baseline estrogen was associated with AD in a few studies, in every trial where estrogen was given, AD decreased.

❂ Aromatase inhibitors: a time for reflection. Birge SJ. *Menopause*. 2007 Nov-Dec;14(6):971-2. Estrogen use decreased coronary calcium, reduced heart attacks by half, and dropped death rate 35 percent if it was started within ten years of the menopause. Lack of estrogen had adverse neurological effects, including 62 percent with memory loss.

❂ Lifelong Estrogen Exposure and Memory in Older Post-menopausal Women. Tierney, M. C., Ryan, J., Ancelin, M.-L., Moieddin, R., Rankin, S., Yao, C., & MacLusky, N. J. (2013). *Journal of Alzheimer's Disease*, 601-608. Hormone therapy protects memory in older women.

❂ Prospective Randomized Trial to Assess Effects of Contin-uing Hormone Therapy on Cerebral Funtion in Postmenopausal Women at Risk for Dementia. Rasgon, N. L., Geist, C. L., Kenna, H. A., Wroolie, T. E., Williams, K. E., & Silverman, D. H. (2014). *PLOS*, 1-10. Hormone therapy protects against cognitive decline. Those who discontinued it had frontal cortex degeneration and worsening brain function. Premarin did not help as much as estradiol.

✪ The Mortality Toll of Estrogen Avoidance: An Analysis of Excess Deaths Among Hysterectomized Women Aged 50 to 59 Years. Sarrel, P. M., Nijike, V. Y., Vinante, V., & Katz, D. L. (2013). *American Journal of Public Health,* e1-e6. Declines in heart disease and cancer reduced death in hormone therapy recipients. Notes that the WHI frightened women away from hormones, which significantly increased many diseases and mortality.

✪ Estrogen and the Brain Beyond ER-Alpha, ER-Beta, and 17 Beta-Estradiol. Toran-Allerand, C. *Columbia University College of Physicians and Surgeons,* 136-137.(2005). Reviews estradiol's favorable influences on brain neurons.

✪ Estrogen and Alzheimer's disease: the story so far. Cholerton, B., Gleason, C., Baker, L., & Asthana, S. (2002). *Drugs Aging.* [PubMed]. Describes estrogen's brain protective role. It improves the mental functioning of women with AD and reduces the risk of AD in normal postmenopausal women.

✪ Estrogens and Alzheimer disease risk; Is there a window of opportunity? Henderson, V. W., & Rocca, W. A. (2012). *Neurology.* Describes how the Women's Health Initiative study distorted estrogen therapy, and how the consensus of the literature supported it before the WHI was published.

✪ Estrogen Neuroprotection and the Critical Period Hypothesis. Scott, E., Zhang, Q.-g., Wang, R., Vadlamudi, R., & Brann, D. (2012). *Front Neuroendocrinol.* If estrogen is given during the critical period in early menopause, many brain problems are prevented.

✪ Neuroprotective effects of 17beta-estradiol and nonfeminizing estrogens against H2O2 toxicity in human neuroblastoma SK-N-SH cells.Wang, X., Dykens, J., Perez, E., Liu, R., Yang, S., Covey, D., & Simpkins, J. (2006). *Mol Pharmacol.* Estrogen protects the human brain according to both laboratory and human studies.

⊗ Mitochondrial mechanisms of estrogen neuroprotection. *Brian* Simpkins, J., & Dykens, I. (2008). *Res Rev.*[PubMed]. Because of information such as the last cited study, estrogen is likely useful to treat AD and other brain diseases.

⊗ Lifelong Estrogen Exposure and Memory in Older Post-menopausal Women.Tierney, M. C., Ryan, J., Ancelin, M.-L., Moieddin, R., Rankin, S., Yao, C., & MacLusky, N. J. (2013). *Journal of Alzheimer's Disease*, 601-608. Previous hormone therapy preserves brain function for older women.

⊗ Postmenopausal Hormone Therapy Increases Retinal Blood Flow and Protects the Retinal Nerve Fiber Layer. Desch-enes, M. C., Descovich, D., Moreau, M., Grnager, L., Kuchel, G. A., Mikkola, T. S., . . . Lesk, M. R. (2009). *Investigative Ophthal-mology & Visual Science.* Hormone therapy, particularly estrogen, preserves retinal blood flow. (The retina is considered part of the brain.)

⊗ High-dose estradiol improves cognition for women with AD: results of a randomized study. Asthana, S., Baker, L., Craft, S., Stanczyk, F., Veith, R., Raskind, M., & Plymate, S. (2001). *Neurology.*[PubMed]. Estrogen improves mental functioning in postmenopausal women.

⊗ Cognitive and neuroendocrine response to transdermal estrogen in postmenopausal women with Alzheimer's disease: results of a placebo-controlled, double-blind, pilot study. Asthana, S., Craft, S., Baker, L., Raskind, M., Birnbaum, R., Lofgreen, C., . . . Plymate, S. (1999). *Psychoneuroendocrinology.* Estrogen improves mental function in postmenopausal women with AD.

⊗ Do estradiol levels influence on the cognitive function during antidepressant treatments in post-menopausal women. Pae, C., Mandelli, L., Han, C., Ham, B., Masand , P., Patkar, A., . . . Serretti, A. (2008). *Neuro Endocrinol Lett.*[PubMed]. Estrogen improves mental function, decreases risk of stroke, AD, and heart attacks.

✪ Endogenous Estradiol is Associated with Verbal Memory in Nondemented Older Men. Zimmerman, M. E., Lipton, R. B., Santoro, N., McConnell, D. S., Derby, C. A., Katz, M. J. Saunders-Pullman, R. (2011). *HHS Public Access*. Older men with higher estrogen levels had better mental functioning.

∼

TESTOSTERONE AND BRAIN FUNCTION

✪ Low free testosterone is an independent risk factor for Alzheimer's disease. Hogercorst, Hogervorst, E., Bandelow, S., Combrinck, M., & Smith, A. (2004). *Gerontol*. Low testosterone predicts AD.

✪ Effects of Testosterone on Cognitive and Brain Aging in Elderly Men. Moffat, S. (2005). *N.Y. Academy of Science*. 1055, 80-92. Excellent though dated review article which is hampered by gobbledegook "science" language.

✪ Testosterone improves spatial memory in men with Alzheimer disease and mild cognitive impairment.Cherrier et al. (2005). *Neurology*, 64, 2063-2068. As per the title.

✪ Free testosterone and risk for Alzheimer disease in older men. Moffat SD, Zonderman AB, Metter EJ, et al. *Neurology*. 2004 Jan 27;62(2):188-193. Testosterone levels were lower in men who developed Alzheimer's.

✪ Sex steroids modify working memory. Janowsky J et al. *J Cogn Neurosci* 2000 May;12(3): 407-14. Giving testosterone to men improved memory.

✪ Testosterone reduces neuronal secretion of Alzheimer's beta-amyloid peptides. Gouras GK et al. *Proc Natl Acad Sci USA* 2000 Feb 1; 97(3):1202-5. Testosterone administration prevented manufacture of this AD marker.

✪ Endogenous sex hormones and cognitive function in older men. Barrett-Connor E et al. *J Clin Endocrinol Metab* 1999

Oct;84(10):3681-5s. Testosterone use improved brain function, but not when a blocker was added (anastrozole).

✪ Testosterone reduces neuronal secretion of Alzheimer's beta-amyloid peptides. *Proceedings of the National Academy of Science* (2000). Testosterone reduces production of Alzheimer's brain peptides in both cell cultures and rats.

✪ The Impact of Luteinizing hormone and Testosterone on beta amyloid accumulation: animal and human clinical studies. Verdile, G., Asih, P. R., Barron, A. M., Wahjoepramono, E. J., Ittner, L. M., & Martins, R. N. (2015). *Hormones and Behavior.* Reports the association between AD, mental performance, and testosterone levels in older men. Says that promising human trials show efficacy for treatment.

✪ Effects of testosterone on cognitive and brain aging in elderly men. Moffat, S. (2005). *Ann N Y Acad Sci.*[PubMed]. High levels correlate with mental preservation and low levels with deterioration.

✪ Testosterone and cognitive function: current clinical evidence of a relationship. Beauchet, O. (2006). *Eur J Endocrinol.* Same conclusions as the last article, says that replacement likely helps.

✪ Course and Predictors of Cognitive Function in Patients With Prostate Cancer Receiving Androgen-Deprivation Therapy: A Controlled Comparison. Gonzalez, B. D. Et al (2015). *Journal of Clinical Oncology*, 2021. Testosterone blockers cause mental impairment.

✪ ADT for Prostate Cancer May Up Alzheimer's Risk. Mulcahy, N. (2015). *Medscape Family Medicine.* Testosterone blockers cause AD later.

✪ Endogenous sex hormone levels and cognitive function in aging men: is there an optimal level? Muller, M., Aleman, A., Grobbee, D., de Haan, E., & van der Schouw, Y. (2005). *Neurology.*[PubMed]. Higher testosterone levels correlated with better mental performance at any age.

~

GROWTH HORMONE AND THE BRAIN

✪ Growth Hormone in the brain: Characteristics of Specific Brain Targets for the Hormone and Their Functional Significance. Nyberg F. *Front Neuroendocrinol* 2000 Oct;21(4):330-48. HGH improves brain function, alertness, and motivation.

✪ Insulin-Like Growth Factor-1 and Cognitive Function in Healthy Older Men Aleman A. et al. *J Clin Endocrinol Metab* 84:471-475, 1999. HGH improved brain and social functioning in older men.

✪ Insulin-like Growth Factor-1 (IGF-1) protects cells from apoptosis by Alzheimer's V6421 Mutant Amyloid Precursor protein through IGF-1 receptor in an IGF-binding protein-sensitive manner. Takako Nikura et al. *J Neuroscience*, 2001; 21(6):1902-1910. HGH protects against Alzheimer's amyloid protein buildup.

✪ Relationships between cortisol, dehydroepiandrosterone sulphate and insulin-like growth factor-I system in dementia. Murialdo, G., Barreca, A., Nobili, F., Rollero , A., Timossi, G., Gianelli, M., . . . Polleri, A. (2001). *J Endocrinol*.[PubMed]. AD patients had lower HGH and DHEA levels.

✪ Insulin-Like Growth Factor-I and Insulin-Like Growth Factor Binding Protein-3 in Alzheimer's Disease. Duron, E., Funalot, B., Brunel, N., Coste, B., Quinquis, L., Viollet, C., . . . Hanon, O. (2012). *Endocrine Research*. AD patients had low HGH levels.

✪ Growth hormone, insuline-like growth factor-1 and the aging cardiovascular system. Khan, A., Sane, D., Wannenburg, T., & Sonntag, W. (2002). *Unbound MEDLINE*. Reports that HGH produced muscle improvement, fat reduction, mental improvement, and heart protection.

✪ Update on new therapeutic options for the somatopause. Ceda, G., Dell'Aglio, E., Morganti, S., Denti, L., Maggio, M.,

Lauretani, F., . . . Valenti, G. (2010). *Unbound MEDLINE*. Same conclusions as last reference.

❂ Free Insulin-like growth factor-I and cognitive function in older persons living in the community. Landi, F., Capoluongo, E., Russo, A., Onder, G., Cesari, M., Lulli, P., . . . Bernabei, R. (2007). *Scopus*. HGH is low in older people who have mental decline.

❂ Effects of Growth Hormone-Releasing Hormone on Cognitive Function in Adults With Mild Cognitive Impairment and healthy Older Adults. Baker, L. D., Barsness, S. M., Borson, S., Merriam, G. R., Friedman, S. D., Craft, S., & Vitiello, M. V. (2012). *Arch Neurol*. HGH benefitted healthy older adults.

❂ Can A Growth Hormone-Stimulate Drug Improve Cognitive Function. Fitzgerald, S. (2012). *Neurology Today*, 1, 17-18. Growth hormone releasing factor improved brain functioning.

❂ Potential Non-Growth Uses of rhIGF-I. (2013). *The National Institute of Diabetes and Digestive Kidney Disease.* IGF-1, a natural substance related to HGH, helped the brain eliminate amyloid protein.

❂ Alzeihmer's Disease in Men Linked to Low Levels of Hormone, IGF-1. Chase, C. (2012). *The Endocrine Society*. Low HGH levels, as measured by IGF-1, were linked with mental status and Alzheimer's disease in men.

TRUSTED RESOURCES

My website is RobertYohoAuthor.com. Email me at yoho.
robert@gmail.com.

A basic, unreferenced book for patients is: *How to Achieve
Healthy Aging* by Neal Rouzier, MD.

For steroid-related legal problems, consider Rick Collins,
Esq.: www.cgmbesq.com, rcollins@cgmbesq.com.

Here are additional references and summaries.

Or, see the Sources section at RobertYohoAuthor.com and click
on the top right button, "Hormone References."

You can take Dr. Rouzier's course even if you are not a medical professional. See worldlinkmedical.com to sign up, network, or listen to podcasts. You may be permitted to take the certification exam after you have training.

Here are a few of his lectures for doctors. Estrogen, progesterone, and cancer:

Testosterone:

Estrogen:

Hormones and the brain:

Each of Dr. Rouzier's binders summarizes hundreds of studies.

MEET THE AUTHOR

Robert Yoho in 2010

PROFESSIONAL CV:

✪ 67 years old (2021). Current website: RobertYohoAuthor.com.

✪ Emergency medicine career out of medical school.

✪ American Board of Emergency Medicine: passed board exams and twice re-certified.

✪ Practiced three decades as a cosmetic surgeon, now retired (see DrYoho.com).

American Society of Cosmetic Breast Surgery: fellow, trustee, officer, and past president.

✪ American Board of Cosmetic Surgery: passed board exams and twice re-certified.

✪ Fellow, American Academy of Cosmetic Surgery (inactive).

✪ New Body Cosmetic Surgery Center: founder & director (inactive).

✪ American Association Ambulatory Health Care (AAAHC) accredited surgical/medical practice for over 25 years.

✪ Retired from medical practice in 2019.

CLIMBER CV:

- ✪ El Capitan, Half Dome (Yosemite): 24-hour ascents
- ✪ Free ascents of Astroman (11.c) and Crucifix (12.a)
- ✪ First ascents in Yosemite, Joshua Tree, Devil's Tower
- ✪ Solo ascents to 5.10c

After climbing Yosemite's El Capitan in 26 hours. We
are two MDs and a Ph.D.

MEET ROBERT L. MORGAN, APRN-BC, ACNP, MSN

Owner of Kingwood Health & Wellness Clinic, Houston (Kingwoodwellness.com). Primary focus: hormone and thyroid replacement and treatment of obesity, diabetes, and cardiovascular disease.

Past affiliations: Clear Lake Regional Medical Center: nurse administrator and trainer, including medical/surgical ICU. The University of Texas Medical Branch Hospital: Surgical intensive care unit trainer, manager, resource nurse.

TRAINING AND DEGREES:

Nurse Practitioner, Bachelor's Science Nursing: University of Texas Medical Branch-Galveston (2003).

Board Certified: Acute Care Nurse Practitioner (American Nurses Credentialing Center).

RESEARCH:

Founder, institutional review board, KHW Clinic.

Participant in several studies in thyroid optimization.

Worked on tissue plasminogen activator (tPA) trials for suspected CVA patients at Clear Lake Regional Medical Center.

Graduate school research focus: Analysis of the Women's Health Initiative study regarding hormone replacement therapy.

Collaborator in a thyroid research program to see if optimizing thyroid levels decreased diabetes and cardiovascular disease.

POST-GRADUATE AFFILIATIONS:

Co-founder, American Association of Hormone Specialists

Past president, Texas Peri-anesthesia Nurses Association

Certified in Advanced Bio-Identical Hormone Replacement (World Link Medical).

A current, active member of American Academy of Clinical Endocrinologists, American Academy of Anti-Aging Medicine, American College of Gynecology, North American Menopause Society, Society of Clinical Research Associates, Endocrine Society, Obesity Medicine Association, Association of American Physicians & Surgeons, Academy of Nutrition and Dietetics.

CONSULTING:

Preceptor for hormone care, both physicians and nurse practitioners.

Developed and copyrighted the Thyroid Decision Tank©, a simple way to explain thyroid treatment to other providers.

Proctored a physician collaborator of *Ageless (2006)* by Suzanne Somers.

Robert passed away as this book was published. He was a dear friend who will be sorely missed.

PLEASE STAY IN TOUCH

I hope we now have a relationship. I am distributing this e-book free for a limited time at RobertYohoAuthor.com. If you are not yet reading on an e-reader, the support people at my book distribution service will help you get one and start reading. E-books are easy and help you find references. If you get on my contact list, I will email you more content.

Please make time to write an Amazon review. I will read it, and I appreciate you for doing it. Reviewing a book before finishing is acceptable, and you can update what you say later if you want. Use this link if this is an ebook.

I answer polite questions at yoho.robert@gmail.com. Email if you want me to speak to your group. Mailing address: 99 West California Blvd #50007, Pasadena, CA 91115.

OTHER PUBLICATIONS

✪ *Butchered By "Healthcare"* (2020)
✪ *A New Body in One Day* (2004)
✪ Twenty articles in medical journals, including:

The American Journal of Cosmetic Surgery   Vol. 20, No. 3, 2003   149

Modified Propofol-Ketamine Cosmetic Surgery: Anesthesia Technique for Surgeon-Administered Anesthesia With Particular Reference to Liposuction

Robert Yoho, MD; Kevin Mullen, PA

Review   > Dermatol Surg. 2005 Jul;31(7 Pt 1):733-43; discussion 743.

doi: 10.1097/00042728-200507000-00001.

Review of the liposuction, abdominoplasty, and face-lift mortality and morbidity risk literature

Robert A Yoho [1], Jeremy J Romaine, Deborah O'Neil

ACKNOWLEDGMENTS

Martha Rosenberg encouraged me more than anyone else. She knows medical corruption better than I do because she has been writing about it for decades.

Grant Horner went through the complete document for style issues and encouraged me all the way.

Kris Solem did his usual fantastic work on the audio engineering.

Mark Berman is a mentor and a friend. He has been encouraging and made time to review my project.

Lynne Bateson is a top editor and may be the smartest person in the room.

My daughter Sarah Yoho had the innovative idea of embedding videos and links into QR codes for the print version.

My dear friend Greg Anderson's son took the photo of the shark and scuba diver in the Three Goliaths chapter.

Robert Morgan, APRN, made time to host me in Houston for a week. He explained many arcane details of hormone therapy and also supplied references. He had a better grasp of the academics than anyone but Neal.

My beta readers are fantastic: Tom Lambert, Paul Johnson, Pat Lillis, Denis and Sandy Portero, George Boris, Patrick B. James, Dan Metcalf, Brian Dobrin, Jeff and Ann Martin. If I forgot anyone, sorry and thanks.

This entire project is based on the lifework of Neal Rouzier. He thinks I have taken too hard a position about corporate medicine. My response is that four years of study killed my ability to write about corruption using euphemisms.

$\sim$

MY LAST WORD

I know what you are thinking by now: Why can't the author come up with a nice phrase like, "These changes in the aging phenotype are correlated with a decline in the amplitude of pulsatile growth hormone secretion and the resulting decrease in plasma levels of its anabolic mediator, insulin-like growth factor-1 (IGF-1)."

I will let George Orwell reply. This is from his *Politics and the English Language* essay, which I try to review every few months. I believe it applies to science writing most of all.

> [The English language] becomes ugly and inaccurate [not] because our thoughts are foolish, but the slovenliness of our language makes it easier for us to have foolish thoughts… Modern English, especially written English, is full of bad habits which spread by imitation and which can be avoided if one is willing to take the necessary trouble… modern writing at its worst does not consist in picking out words for the sake of their meaning and inventing images in order to make the meaning clearer. It consists in gumming together long strips of words which have already been set in order by someone else and making the results presentable by sheer humbug.